FINE LIVING

130 Designs with Master Suites, Grand Kitchens, Media Rooms, and More

FINE LIVING

130 HOME DESIGNS WITH LUXURY AMENITIES

Published by Home Planners, LLC
Wholly owned by Hanley-Wood, LLC
3275 W. Ina Road, Suite 220
Tucson, Arizona 85741

DISTRIBUTION CENTER
29333 Lorie Lane
Wixom, Michigan 48393

President, Jayne Fenton
Chief Financial Officer, Joe Carroll
Vice President, Publishing, Jennifer Pearce
Vice President, General Manager, Marc Wheeler
Executive Editor, Linda Bellamy
National Sales Manager, Book Division, Julie Marshall
Managing Editor, Jason D. Vaughan
Special Projects Editor, Kristin Schneidler
Editor, Nate Ewell
Associate Editor, Kathryn R. Sears
Lead Plans Associate, Morenci C. Clark
Plans Associates, Jill M. Hall, Elizabeth Landry, Nick Nieskes
Proofreaders/Copywriters, Douglas Jenness, Sarah Lyons
Technical Specialist, Jay C. Walsh
Lead Data Coordinator, Fran Altemose
Data Coordinators, Misty Boler, Melissa Siewert
Production Director, Sara Lisa
Production Manager, Brenda McClary

BIG DESIGNS, INC.
President, Creative Director, Anthony D'Elia
Vice President, Business Manager, Megan D'Elia
Vice President, Design Director, Chris Bonavita
Editorial Director, John Roach
Assistant Editor, Tricia Starkey
Director of Design and Production, Stephen Reinfurt
Group Art Director, Kevin Limongelli
Photo Editor, Christine DiVuolo
Art Director, Jessica Hagenbuch
Graphic Designer, Mary Ellen Mulshine
Graphic Designer, Lindsey O'Neill-Myers
Graphic Designer, Jacque Young
Assistant Photo Editor, Brian Wilson
Project Director, David Barbella
Assistant Production Manager, Rich Fuentes

PHOTO CREDITS

Front Cover & Opposite: Design HPT9700123 by ©The Sater Design Collection.
For details, see page 62. Photo by ©Laurence Taylor Photography.

Back Cover: Design HPT9700002 by ©Home Design Services, Inc.
For details, see page 52. Photo by Everett & Soule.

Back Cover Inset: Design HPT9700123 by ©The Sater Design Collection.
For details, see page 62. Photo by ©Laurence Taylor Photography.

10 9 8 7 6 5 4 3 2 1

Printed in the United States of America

Library of Congress Catalog Card Number: 2003113856

ISBN: 1-931131-24-4

60

62

48

FINE LIVING

130 HOME DESIGNS WITH
LUXURY AMENITIES

Ideas & Inspiration

Portfolio of Home Plans

Today's kitchens are more often common sitting areas in addition to cooking centers.

CATER TO YOUR NEEDS

Plan ahead to make your kitchen great before you build

WRITTEN BY PAULETTE DAGUE

You've seen them on the Web and in magazines—those utterly fabulous kitchens where it looks as though gourmet meals practically create themselves. Whether your tastes run to French Country or ultra-modern, you can have a remarkable kitchen that is a dream to work in. The key? Serious planning before you start building. All kitchens generally have the same elements: storage, work surfaces, fixtures, and appliances. It's how these elements are arranged and how many of them are included that make the difference between nice and nightmare. Begin by identifying your specific needs in a kitchen.

BELOW: Remember to allow for a workspace in your kitchen for paying bills and organizing records. **RIGHT:** Separate seating areas create a greater sense of space and enhance kitchen efficiency.

■ How many people will be using the kitchen—in particular, how many cooks might be working simultaneously? If more than one, you may want to consider multiple work areas, or at least a main sink and a prep sink with adjacent counter space.

■ Is there a need for universal design in your kitchen? The kitchen is the one area of the home that is the most difficult to navigate for anyone with limitations. Overly high counters, unreachable controls, hard-to-turn faucet levers, and many other obstacles can be overcome if you work accessible features into your kitchen.

■ How much do you and your family use the kitchen and for what sort of cooking? If you're a gourmet cook, you probably have ideas about the kind of appliances and details you want—perhaps a convection oven for baking, or a built-in griddle for Sunday-morning pancakes. If, however, you only cook occasionally your needs may be more spartan.

■ What about eating space in the kitchen? Do you need a table and chairs or do you use a formal dining room most of the time and only need a snack counter? Incorporate only what you really think you'll need to minimize floor area and maximize work space.

■ Storage is always a problem—especially in the kitchen. Take good inventory of what you now store in your current kitchen and consider what you'd like in the new one. Will you need secure storage for dangerous chemicals and cleaners? Do you need to store hobby products? How do you handle small appliances—do you like them exposed on the counter or tucked away in an appliance garage?

■ What kind of entertaining do you like to do and how often do you entertain? If you and your family are casual entertainers, you may prefer an open kitchen that connects with a great room or family room so there is easy transition from one area to the other. If more formal affairs are the norm for you, you'll want the kitchen to have easy access to the dining room, maybe via a butler's pantry or wet bar.

■ Besides cooking, what other activities will likely take place in the kitchen? Homework? Entertaining? Household business? TV watching? Pet feeding? Sewing? Think about all the things you do in the kitchen now and plan to build your new kitchen to accommodate them.

LOCATION

For best efficiency, the kitchen should be located in an area that will avoid general traffic through it, while remaining convenient to dining and living areas. You'll also want to consider outside access to a garage for easy unloading of groceries and to a backyard for barbecues.

ROOM ARRANGEMENT

Like other rooms in the home, the kitchen may be built in any number of shapes. However, three basic arrangements predominate for efficiency:

Corridor or Galley—with facing walls of appliances, cabinets, and work surfaces. This shape is great for small kitchens as it best uses available space. However, it does not allow for a table and chairs in the kitchen.

U-shaped—which keeps the work centers in easy reach and eliminates through traffic. There are many variations of this shape, some with peninsula extensions for a snack bar.

L-shaped—similar to the U-shaped kitchen, this configuration is handy, especially for homes where two cooks may be working at the same time.

To really make the most of L- and U-shaped kitchens, consider a work island, which may contain a rangetop, prep sink, or just a work surface.

No matter what shape a kitchen has, it should be designed around the gold standard for kitchen efficiency—the work triangle. This time-honored principle examines the distance between the sink, range, and refrigerator (a triangle) as a basis for good placement.

The principle holds that the total distance of the triangle should be no more than 26 feet and that no leg of the triangle should be more than 9 feet or less than 4 feet. A work triangle total of less than 12 feet is unlikely to have sufficient counter and storage space. If two cooks are working together, then there should be a triangle for each. One leg of the triangle can be shared, but the two should not cross.

The National Kitchen & Bath Association outlines specific guidelines for kitchen layout and other pertinent details. To review their guidelines, visit www.nkba.org. ■

SUITE DREAMS

*Go ahead, be selfish. With careful planning
you can make this space your own private sanctuary*

WRITTEN BY MARY KELLY SELOVER

It's a dirty little secret. Homeowners undertaking new construction or a major remodel often give the master suite short shrift. What drives them to commit this silly sin? Surprisingly, it's usually the desire to be unselfish. Most homeowners lavish time and attention—not to mention tens of thousands of dollars—on the kitchen and family room. They rationalize that children, relatives, and friends will all enjoy and share this space. What they forget to account for is just how much time they, the homeowners, will actually spend in their bedroom and bath. Take a moment to tote up the average time you spend grooming, dressing, and sleeping, including TV and reading time if you tend to undertake these activities on your Serta. You'll probably realize that the master suite accounts for the lion's share of hours you spend in your own home. So what's greedy about allocating extra square footage and budget dollars to the space you frequent so often; where it's possible to create a refuge from the hubbub of the world just beyond your door? Nothing. Now is the time, at the very beginning of the planning process, to think about the numerous ways you will use the space, and to begin listing personal preferences for everything from the lavatory to the lighting.

LEFT: Rather than the usual linen closet, the homeowners chose an attractive armoire for storage of towels and sundries.
RIGHT: A tester bed, undraped, makes a small room appear larger. Wool carpet looks like sisal but is barefoot friendly.

Start your planning in the bathroom, since plumbing has to be worked out as part of the overall blueprint. Make a list of your likes and dislikes. For example, is it important to you that the toilet have its own compartment with a door? Do you want to sacrifice square footage for a large jetted tub or would you rather have a two-person shower with multiple sprays? Are two sinks a must for you in a shared bath?

You'll also need to think about storage. If you choose pedestals or wall-mounted sinks you'll need to accommodate for the lack of vanities with a closet, armoire, or medicine cabinet to hide personal items. If you like to shave or apply makeup in front of a mirror over a sink, it's a good idea to position task lighting here, preferably with a dimmer for flattering control. Would you prefer your bath be large enough for a chair or a bench? And would you be willing to sacrifice space in the adjacent bedroom to do so?

Planning the bath of a master suite really comes down to deciding what matters to you most and how to make it work in the floor plan. Don't take no for an answer from your architect or your contractor until you are completely satisfied that what you really want can't somehow be squeezed in.

Once you've decided on all these elements, the time has come to select faucets and other fixtures as well as surface treatments, including tile, paint, wallcoverings, even carpet. Each will further contribute to the style of the bath as well as to the adjacent bedroom—since both spaces should work harmoniously as a whole. The architecture of your house most likely will guide your choices. A minimal, modernist-style bath would look completely out of place in a Colonial or Victorian home, and vice versa.

This said, the master suite should be the most personal, even idiosyncratic space in your house. It's your private domain where you have no one to please but yourself. Here is the place for mementos, photos, and quirky much-loved objects, as long as they don't detract from the atmosphere of relaxation and serenity that is your ultimate goal.

Refrain from creating a home office in the master suite unless you can cleverly tuck it away behind closed doors. (Having a computer station or a desk covered with bills, mail, and files is a constant reminder of work waiting to be done. It absolutely wreaks havoc with your haven!)

Ideally, in the master bedroom, all the senses are catered to. Think

LEFT: The corner wall-mounted sink conserves valuable floor space in a small bath. Double-hung shutters complement this space's straight-forward, unfussy look.

RIGHT: Out of sight, out of mind. A compact office, complete with bookshelves and file storage, tucks conveniently into the corner of this master bedroom.

Ornate side-by-side pedestal sinks, a wood-rimmed antique-style tub, and a fan-backed garden chair set a Victorian tone. Practicality reigns, however. The oak floor has been coated with marine polyurethane to protect against water damage; the well-lit mirrors are adjustable.

about what provides ease both awake and asleep. Do you like the sun to wake you to start your day? Then sheer curtains are a good choice for you. But what about your partner? Those who prefer a very dark room would do well to line curtains with black-out fabric. It's these kinds of issues that call for compromise. In any event, be sure to have your builder position windows to make the most of your view while still maintaining privacy and maximizing airflow when they are opened.

Adequate storage in the master suite is key to its design. Fitted closets, customized to your own wardrobe, have become increasingly popular and are a step above a walk-in closet. No matter the size of your suite, be sure to allot ample room for clothing and accessories.

Many new master suites boast reading/media areas with bookshelves, TVs and stereos, upholstered chairs, and lamps. Some homeowners even incorporate small breakfast alcoves with a cof-

feemaker and a mini-fridge into their plans. Others carve out space for exercise equipment or yoga mats.

However, what's most important is the bed. Almost always, it is the room's focal point, and no matter its design, should complement the scale of the space. Last but not least, be sure to spring for a truly comfortable mattress, perfect pillows, and luxurious linens. After all, you've worked hard to create your own special master suite. You deserve to rest, blissfully, on your laurels. ■

BATHS & BEYOND
*The pros tell all, from the best layouts to
the most sought-after accents*

Architects, designers, and builders are different from you and me. In idle moments, we think about the score of last night's Little League game or maybe what we'll fix for tomorrow's dinner. These creative types, however, are more likely to ponder where to site a window or how best to lay wall tile. It seems they just can't stop thinking about ways to make each new project better than their last. The professionals interviewed on the following pages are no exception. And because all of their work is custom, over the years they've accommodated hundreds of special requests from clients, requests that have forced them to think in original, creative ways and to devise superior solutions.

ABOVE: Raised vanities and radiant floor heating add to the comfort level of this master bath by Peter Stoner.

LEFT: Porcelain tile in a matte finish mimics weathered sandstone for a rustic look in a weekend house by Dick Jordan. **BELOW:** The pale-toned cabinetry and countertop are in sync with similar paneling in the master bath. **OPPOSITE TOP:** The Stoner-designed maple vanity includes a built-in bar for keeping hand towels ready. **OPPOSITE BOTTOM:** Light is prevalent in this Peter Stoner bath, as French doors topped by matching transom reveal a bath with a 13-foot peaked ceiling.

It's no surprise, then, that since the bath is the most personal space in the house, that it is also the focus of many of these ingenuities and wish-list items. Over time these experts have come to know which are truly worthwhile; they share their thoughts here. What besides comforting and convenient extras sets a bathroom apart? According to the pros: a well-conceived layout and attention to architectural detail. Both figure strongly in the baths on the following pages.

So whether you are renovating an existing space or creating a bath from scratch, take heed. There's lots of useful insider information to come that will benefit you and be a boon for your bath.

DICK JORDAN [BUILDER]

In business for 20 years, builder and developer Dick Jordan, principal of Brainard Ridge Associates of Windham, New York, specializes in custom timber-frame construction. Hundreds of townhouses, condos, and private homes at the Windham Mountain Ski Resort attest to his experience and practiced eye. Several of his signature touches can be found in the 8-by-12-foot master bath of the weekend getaway (above left).

■ **Water closet.** This compartment with toilet provides maximum privacy in a His and Hers bath. Its pocket door is a space-saver.

■ **Spacious shower enclosure.** When square footage permits, Jordan likes to specify stalls that can easily accommodate two people. This 6-by-4-foot example boasts two built-in benches. Tucked away behind the tub, it requires no shower door or curtain.

■ **Rainhead fixture.** Ceiling-mounted in the shower, this luxurious feature provides a cloudburst-like soaking.

■ **Minimal tile pattern.** This reinforces the "natural, country look" Jordan says his clients prefer. For the shower floor, the tile has been laid on the diagonal for subtle contrast.

■ **Heated towel bar.** Jordan says that after a cold day on the slopes, homeowners really appreciate the pleasure of a warmed terry wrapper.

■ **Large mirror.** "I don't like medicine cabinets," says Jordan. Instead, in most of the

baths he designs, an "uninterrupted expanse of mirror runs above a vanity fitted with lots of drawers."

PETER STONER [ARCHITECT]

In Seattle, Washington, architect Peter Stoner has been renovating and constructing new homes for 24 years. As part of a three-story addition for a circa-1920s Craftsman-style house, he created a master bedroom that opens to a 6-by-20-foot bath (opposite right). This space showcases several notions he employs routinely in his work.

■ **Multiple light sources.** Stoner placed a window in the peaked gable to bring more natural light into the space. Wall sconces offer a decorative touch. However, it's the high-intensity MR-16 ceiling-mounted fixtures directed at the sink bowls that allow for perfect makeup application and the closest of shaves.

■ **Vanity height.** Because it is a master suite used only by adults, Stoner raised the counter height to 36 inches. "I think this is more comfortable for most people," he says.

■ **Bump-out counter.** Bulging at center and receding at the sides, the shape of this tiled counter allows users to stand closer to the sinks and mirrors than is customary.

■ **Radiant floor heating.** "In most of the baths I design, I like to add a separate thermostat and control for the floor," says Stoner. "With a timer, you can set it to begin heating before you wake up in the morning."

■ **Hidden electrical outlets.** Typically, Stoner locates electrical plugs inside a vanity drawer or behind a cabinet door.

■ **Floor-to-ceiling cabinets.** Rather than mounting medicine cabinets over sinks, Stoner often creates required storage by positioning recessed cabinet space between wall studs.

VAL FLORIO [ARCHITECT]

Having worked for a large architectural firm for many years, Val Florio, AIA, was eager to hang up his own shingle. In September 2001, he did just that in Sag Harbor, New York. For the master bath of a newly constructed farmhouse-style residence he designed in Bridgehampton, a neighboring town, Florio eschewed "frilly millwork" and included elements that he says "appeal to Everyman."

■ **Wainscot.** "I use it often in projects," says Florio. "It's a nice simple detail that adds character and goes hand in hand with the style of houses I like to design."

■ **Cubby storage.** This can make up for some of the vanity storage sacrificed to the pedestal sink. Building an open storage section is not expensive, he says, and adds a measure of quality.

■ **Frameless glass shower door.** A stall shower with this kind of unobtrusive-looking door works in any style of bath, according to Florio.

■ **Wood floor.** This is a good choice as long as it's for an adult bath. (Children splash too much.) "Wood is user-friendly once it's stained and sealed with polyurethane," he says. On one occasion, Florio stained oak planks a dark chocolate brown.

Tried and true design tips to make the most of your bathroom

"It's very rich and adds visual warmth," Florio says.

■ **Seasonal accessories.** Changing the color of towels with the seasons, and perhaps adding a sisal rug during winter months, Florio suggests, will keeps this bath's appearance fresh.

THOMAS MOORE [DESIGNER]

New-home construction occupies most of Brewster, Massachusetts, designer Thomas Moore's time. For 15 years he has plied his trade seeking to give the client exactly what he or she wants. He does, however, offer several of his tried and true suggestions for bathrooms.

■ **Sight line.** "Whenever possible, position the toilet so it cannot be seen from the doorway," Moore says. If necessary, build a half-wall for privacy.

■ **Deep drawers.** Because they can accommodate a wider variety of objects, from coffeemakers to compacts, drawers with depth make a practical choice as in the renovated bath of this 50-year-old Cape-style home (below right).

■ **Mirror-mounted lighting.** From a design perspective, this is a clean, streamlined solution to positioning a fixture. It's an especially good solution when space is tight.

■ **Whirlpool tub.** This is an amenity that most of Moore's clients ask for, even in small baths. "I try to oblige, if at all possible," he says. With more shapes and sizes now available, the task has become much easier.

■ **Washer and dryer.** In many baths, space can be found to hide a stacked washer/dryer behind a door that is louvered for additional ventilation. Locate the unit in a bathroom on the level of the house that has most of the bedrooms. Then, used bed linens and towels are closer to where they will be cleaned. ■

ABOVE: Bright white wainscot—a favored element of Val Florio—makes this bath crisp. **RIGHT:** Sight lines are key to Thomas Moore, as seen by the stark white walls and cabinetry here, which enhance the clean lines and cleaned-up look of this well-ordered bath.

A GREAT INVESTMENT

*Improving your master suite will do more than just add luxury
to your life—it will add value to your home*

WRITTEN BY DIANE S. COURTNEY

If you've been feeling deprived by the sight of all the luxurious bathrooms that grace the pages of design magazines—and your friends' homes!—don't torture yourself a second longer. Remodeling or adding a new bath to your house is not just an indulgence: Rather, it will bring value to your home. In Remodeling magazine's "Cost vs. Value Report" online, "Does Remodeling Pay?", one real-estate agent says, "Clients who have their bathrooms remodeled for between $10,000 and $15,000 usually recoup all of that [on resale]." Consider the statistics: As a national average, $9,786 spent on a bathroom remodel has a resale value of $7,955—81 percent of the job cost. Even more important if you're considering selling your house, a remodeled bath could make the difference between a sale and a walkaway. Adding a new bath can be even more advantageous, because buyers are looking for more baths today than older homes tend to provide. Also, buyers' expectations are often set by new construction, where bathrooms are big and rife with luxurious amenities. And resale value aside, renovating or adding a luxurious bath directly impacts how you experience your home. In recent years, the bath has become so large and luxurious that today's homeowners often use it as a wonderfully private and restorative retreat. Celebrities Michelle Pfeiffer and Trudie Styler have been quoted as saying they even use their master baths for business meetings. But whether you plan to floss or fax in your new space, careful planning is the key to a beautiful bath. The four bathrooms that follow take distinctly different approaches to bathroom luxury, but all use classic design basics—light, views, color, and architectural style—to great effect. Let them inspire you to fulfill your dream—and improve your investment.

This luxurious His and Hers bath is only connected by the shower, which has a door on either end, and the window over the whirlpool tub.

BRIGHT OUTLOOK

A pale palette and plenty of streaming sunlight unite
the two halves of this luxurious double bath

For second homeowners arriving in sunny Vero Beach, Florida, from a gray and dreary Northeast winter, light-filled interiors are a big attraction. So the design team from Spectrum Interior Design created a scheme that would give this house in the Orchid Island Golf & Beach Club an airy, casual ambiance appropriate to its resort setting. But when it came to the bath, they faced a challenge: Naturally they wanted to continue the open and airy effect in the master bath, but limited room for windows and close proximity to neighbors meant they'd have to improvise.

Though the bath would not enjoy the ample glazing found in the rest of the house, the designers could create a cohesive look by extending other aspects of their plan into this room.

For instance, the bathroom plays on the home's "Anglo-Caribbean" architecture with elements like the plantation-blind-covered windows that provide both light and privacy and the contrast of dark wood against pale-colored walls.

And, since in a bathroom there is ample opportunity to concentrate on materials that create an impression of brightness, the designers made their choices work doubly hard. The shining marble surfacing, large expanses of glass—both in the shower stall and mirrored vanities—and the glossy white woodwork all reflect light, creating an impression of brightness. Darker elements—the vanity cabinetry, the towel

caddy, and the picture frame, for instance—ground the room visually.

Overall, despite the lack of windows, the effect is sunny and spacious—a testament to what you can accomplish with some sleight-of-hand design tricks. ∎

PUTTING COLOR TO WORK

Color can create many different effects: comforting, soothing, or invigorating, to name a few. The bath here is a great example of what light, watery shades can do—but that's just a beginning. By contrast, choosing a warm palette with earthy shades in the red and brown families, along with wood tones and some coppery accents, will create a cozy feeling. Energetic colors like clear yellows and leafy greens will have a refreshing appeal.

Also, color can mask architectural defects. To "lift" a low ceiling, paint it a shade lighter than the walls; or, "lower" the ceiling and make the room cozier by painting the ceiling in a dark, warm tone. You can improve the proportions of a long, narrow room by painting the narrow end walls a lighter color than the side walls.

But most important, feel free to experiment: Color is fun!

In the bath's "his" half, dark wood contrasts nicely with the pale-blue walls. Innovative glazing—fixed panes above the vanity and in the wall that connects the spaces—admits light to a windowless area.

SMALL WONDER

Careful planning and a dose of chic
combine in a creative master bath

A master bathroom doesn't have to be huge to become the peaceful haven you crave. Although small, this bath has almost Zen-like tranquility, thanks to its simple, clutter-free aesthetics. But it was clever planning and careful attention to the architecture that makes the compact space so successful.

First, when working with a small space, it's of primary importance to consider flow and function. A well-designed bathroom should meet your needs day-in and day-out and soothe your soul in the process. To arrive at a fresh design that's successful for you, think about your daily routine, as well as the elements of your current bathroom that fall short of your requirements. Then, plan accordingly. If, for example, two people will be sharing the bathroom consider the basic storage requirements needed to maintain a clutter-free, calming space. In the bath pictured here, the homeowners chose a compact but handsome vanity that provides plenty of storage, so both spouses feel organized in their personal grooming areas.

Another important strategy in creating a feeling of calm in a small space is to keep colors quiet and closely related in tone; a single contrasting accent—like the dark countertop in this bath—will add a bold edge. Let lots of light flow in and keep the room's colors neutral to allow for enhanced light. Accents, such as vibrant towels, can bring in any additional color.

Finally, to make the room personal yet still visually relaxing, put out just a few good accessories in eye-pleasing order while keeping all utilitarian clutter behind closed doors.

With a little creativity—and a bit of restraint—a small space can be as efficient as it is elegant. ∎

Spare and sleek, this master bath boasts all the comfort of a larger space but has a scale better suited to convenience and calm.

POINT OF VIEW

*A stunning riverside site sets the stage for
this Victorian-style master bath*

Sometimes, bath design is determined less by the constraints of a house than by the attributes of its site. Case in point: This master bath, which perches high on a cliff above the Hudson River, took its cues from the astounding views first, and from the turn-of-the-century style of the home's architecture second.

Framing the major attraction—the panorama of the mighty Hudson—are grand double-hung windows with arching eyebrows above. And in an inspired bit of space planning, the view is doubled by its reflection in the wide mirrored wall across from the windows above the sinks. The result is a space with glass, light, and views everywhere you turn, a sun-drenched room that imparts a great sense of well-being to its occupants.

To continue the Victorian-style architecture of the house into the master suite, the architect chose Carrera marble, a gray-veined Italian stone widely used in the late 19th century, as much for its practical elegance as for its architecturally appropriate appearance. Handsome, weighty woodwork painted a glossy white and simple white fixtures create an impression of quiet luxury, stunning but never showy. Like well-chosen pieces of jewelry, the faucets and fittings complete the period look, without stealing the show from the star: the fabulous view.

The result is a very special bathroom that lives up to its spectacular setting high above the historic Hudson River—just as it was designed to. ∎

BELOW LEFT: Windows can emphasize (or de-emphasize) views and lend architectural authenticity to your space.
BELOW: The double vanity is surfaced with the same Carrera marble that surrounds the tub.

PAST PRESENT

A well-considered addition creates a brand-new bath that's clearly in keeping with its architectural surroundings

When the owners of a 1926 Seattle bungalow decided they wanted to enlarge their charming nest, they were also determined not to compromise its appealing Craftsman-like character. They had thought of adding a second story, but their architects convinced them that the best strategy was to build a two-story addition, which would allow a very private master suite above.

Still, they wanted a cozy feeling built into the new space. So they kept the rooms small and simple but used architectural elements like high ceilings and transom windows to give an airy quality. The design of the master bath flows from this aesthetic: The spare wood cabinetry is both the dominant design element and the practical backbone of the space, providing plenty of storage and grooming room for two. Architecturally, a four-square theme defines the space, with mirrors balancing cabinet door panels, square panes of glass in the French doors and transom windows, square windows over the tub, and square floor tiles.

In keeping with the Craftsman-like flavor, simple forms were paired with rich materials, as in the handsome maple vanity. Accessories were kept sparse and in line with the architectural motif, with no superfluous ornamentation.

Inspired glazing allows the luxury of sunlit interiors. Two small windows in the bathing area pop open, inviting sun, soft breezes, and the soothing rustle of trees. And simply framed mirrors reflect that light across the room for an appealing openness.

Now the owners enjoy a bath that's in character with their house while giving them all-new convenience and comfort. ∎

SPA STYLE

Your own personal spa? It may be as close as your nearest bathroom

"Life moves at a much faster pace than it did 20 years ago," says Kim Kennedy of Kennedy Designs, Inc., in San Anselmo, California. "Many of us are realizing that having a home retreat for rejuvenation is one of the ways we maintain good health and take care of ourselves." And, she adds, "as spa resorts become increasingly popular as vacation destinations, more and more homeowners are looking to incorporate some of those same features into their homes to enjoy every day."

Topping Kennedy's list of the most requested home spa features are steam showers, exercise areas, fireplaces, soaking tubs, heated floors, and luxurious "hydrowalls" where, at the touch of a button, sheets of water softly cascade over opaque glass to create privacy.

FINDING THE SPACE

Start planning your retreat by considering the space you have, as well as the amenities you want to include. Generally, a home spa offers a space for grooming and hygiene, along with areas devoted to relaxation or exercise, depending upon your individual preferences.

Laura Meyer, one of Kennedy's clients, wanted a quiet corner of her own for reading and relaxing at the end of the day. "I grew up in a large family where privacy was unheard of and am now the mother of four young children. Needless to say, I went to Kim with a strong desire to have a small corner of the world that was entirely mine," says Meyer. By reallocating space in the Meyer bath, Kennedy was able to transform a walk-in closet into a cozy retreat that offered a chaise lounge, built-in bookcase, and small fountain. "A glass brick wall and

skylight kept the space from feeling too confining," says Kennedy. The result? "It's changed my life," says Meyer. "Just knowing that I have a place nearby to get away from everything, even for a few minutes, has given me a fresh, new perspective." She adds, "What amazes me is that something so simple could change my entire outlook."

A LAYOUT YOU'LL LOVE

Architect Lionel Morrison, of Morrison, Seifert, Murphy in Dallas, Texas, has observed a shift in the allocation of space away from the bedroom and into the bath over the last several years. "It makes sense to do a great bath and a smaller bedroom area," says Morrison. "It is a more efficient use of space." Many of Morrison's clients look to him to create a master bath or retreat that is large enough for two people to share comfortably.

THE RIGHT LIGHTING

Illumination holds the key to unlocking the potential of every room, and a home spa is no exception. Natural light, spilling through a skylight or filtered through glass blocks, softens a room and creates an ideal backdrop for any retreat. Morrison prefers to bring in light from the outdoors by adding glass windows and walls or skylights to "bathe" the rooms he designs in natural light. If access to daylight is a problem, he advises "borrowing" light from an adjoining area by creating a wall of sandblasted glass, which allows light to pass through from another room without compromising privacy.

Artificial light should be ambient, and it should blend with the overall mood of the room. Dimmer switches on all lights allow

you to control the amount of illumination in the room by function and by area: brighter for dressing, softer for bathing.

SERENE STYLE

Organic, earthy materials and soft, watery colors establish a soothing palette. Honed sandstone, travertine, limestone, and translucent marbles provide texture and depth in neutral tones for floors and countertops. Likewise, good colors to consider for home spas are those evocative of earth and water. Subtle blues, greens, and warm sand tones create a serene and tranquil setting to soothe the eye and calm the spirit. ∎

NATURAL BEAUTY

For most, the simplicity, balance, and constant regeneration found in nature offer an inspired source of renewal. Bringing the outside in, or opening your retreat to the outdoors reinforces your relationship with the natural world and captures the essence of the spa experience. To accomplish this, many designers use doors or sliding window walls that open onto a private garden.

Whenever possible, take advantage of surrounding gardens, interesting landscapes, or panoramic vistas to set the natural tone of your spa. Or, if you are limited by space, budget, and access to the outdoors, consider a small fountain, plants, or a garden statue to replicate the look and feel of the outdoors.

GLASS HOUSES

*Abundant light, views, and more living space
are just a few of the attractions a sunroom addition has to offer*

WRITTEN BY SUSAN B. HILLSTROM

A couple of centuries ago, sunroom-type structures brightened the homes of only the very rich. Sun-splashed solariums or conservatories created a summer atmosphere indoors, provided places for elegant entertaining, perhaps with a chamber orchestra playing in the background, and acted as greenhouses for nurturing exotic plants. Today, things are more democratic—everyone can enjoy the year-round delights of a room made of glass. There's something for everyone—and for every budget. Offering a big bang for your remodeling buck, sunroom additions move us closer to nature, providing supplemental living space that focuses on light and views, and dissolve the boundary between indoors, and out all year long. One of these glass rooms can also improve the overall look of a house by transforming an unsightly concrete patio, rickety back porch, or plain old blank wall into a handsome architectural feature. So whether you'd like a dramatic solarium with soaring walls of glass and a cathedral-style ceiling or a simple, glass-lined breakfast nook, you'll find yourself making a good investment—both in terms of long-term enjoyment and resale value—in your home. To learn more, turn the page.

Consider the style of your house
before choosing a sunroom, then select materials
that will complement adjoining rooms and outdoor areas

ABOVE: The owners of this home used a combination of fixed window units to create a tailored, Craftsman-style sunroom; natural stone flooring and simple wood furnishings complete the crisp look.

Essentially, contemporary sunrooms are like any other room in your house. They have fully insulated walls and ceilings, insulated-glass windows, systems to provide both heating and cooling, and a door to close them off from adjoining rooms. And they're constructed pretty much the same way, too: The site is excavated, a foundation poured, floor, walls, and roof are framed, and existing walls are opened

up for interior doors or passageways.

Most sunrooms have solid roofs and three walls of glass, but glass-roofed units are becoming popular; and, with a custom sunroom, anything is possible. Jim Ruppel, communications director for Four Seasons Sunrooms in Holbrook, New York, says, "The possibilities range from a simple glass-enclosed bump-out to a sky's-the-limit structure."

PLANNING YOUR PROJECT

Do some homework before plunging into a sunroom project. Think carefully about how you would use the proposed room. Will it become a sitting area, dining space, kitchen addition, an enclosure for a hot tub, a sunny spot for growing plants? Or a combination of several of these? From this brainstorming session will emerge a picture of the kind of sunroom that's right for you.

Also consider placement. One wall of your sunroom should face south to capture maximum winter sun. Some industry experts say a position with walls facing south and east is optimum because it captures sun in the early morning, when temperatures are generally cool, and shuns late-afternoon western sun, which in summer is the hottest. You'll also want to orient your sunroom to the prettiest views on your property; and you may want to nestle it near some leafy deciduous trees to deflect summer heat. In winter, these same trees will lose their leaves and allow sun to penetrate. Existing decks or porches are often used as sunroom sites—a money-saving choice if solid foundations are already in place. Second-floor sunrooms often occupy the space above a garage.

Now is also the time to develop a rough budget. Though manufacturers are unable to provide precise prices, they estimate sunrooms at anywhere from $8,000 all the way to perhaps $100,000 or more, depending on size, materials, and complexity. Or as Mike Probach, sales manager for Lindal Sunrooms, puts it, "The cost is roughly comparable to any simple room addition." If that comparison means nothing to you, ask your local building authority for the average cost per square foot of new construction in your area, then multiply that times the proposed square footage of your addition. It's rough, but it will help you budget your project.

One more thing: Check with your local building code officer about setback restrictions, which affect most residential property and which may restrict the size and placement of your glass room.

MAKING A CHOICE

According to Four Seasons' Jim Ruppel, there are two ways to proceed with shopping. One, become familiar with product lines by visiting the showrooms of sunroom

BELOW LEFT: The combination of expansive glazing and a sloped, wood-paneled ceiling creates an interesting interplay of texture in this family room. **BELOW RIGHT:** Divided-light, picture, and arched units mix well for a traditional effect. **BELOW BOTTOM RIGHT:** It's easy to create a wall of light using standard windows, like the divided-light units shown here.

ABOVE TOP: This classic peaked design lends the instant charm of a Victorian greenhouse. **ABOVE RIGHT:** Also consider landscaping: A meandering path such as this one adds welcoming appeal. **ABOVE:** Because a sunroom addition is linked to both the interior and exterior of your home, entrances and exits are important design features. Here, an arched doorway creates a dramatic introduction to the solarium beyond.

Like any other addition, a solarium must be in proportion to both architectural and landscaping features

dealers and looking over their literature. Find the models you like, then ask a sales rep or design consultant to visit and assess your site. Or, start with an on-site visit, review your needs and property with the consultant, and then choose your model and style.

Most sunrooms are installed by local contractors trained by the manufacturer or by crews that work for the dealer. Once you've ordered the room and had the foundation poured, it takes a few days to a few weeks, says Ruppel, for your ideas to become reality.

If yours is to be a unique or complex project, or part of a larger expansion of

your home, you may want to use an architect to help you with the design and to supervise the construction. Or you can submit your ideas to the manufacturer, who may be able to help you customize a unit to meet your needs.

This is the approach Glenn Atwell took for an attachment to his Tudor-style house in Buffalo, New York. Atwell, an avid gardener, wanted to enjoy his rose garden from inside the house as well as outside. But because of the way the garage sat, there were no windows overlooking it. "However, on top of the garage there was an ugly deck that I never used," Atwell says, "and I thought I could put a sun-

Choose the style of sunroom glazing
with an eye to the views; Here,
divided-light windows would detract
from the dramatic beach vista.

*If your budget is as expansive as your imagination,
the sky is literally the limit when it comes to design options,
so think big, bright and bold—you'll love the dramatic results*

room there." With the help of design consultants from a Four Seasons showroom, Atwell's idea took shape and a large sunroom now sits atop the garage, surveying the garden and providing year-round living space.

If setback restrictions limit the size of your addition, or you don't want to spring for a full sunroom, take heart. Some manufacturers will help you design a small sunsplashed area that adds light and views without significantly expanding space. Fred Foster, a staff architect with Andersen Windows, has helped many customers design such sunny nooks. "Even if you don't have much to work with, you can greatly brighten your existing house by simply replacing a solid wall with glass doors and large windows," says Foster. Creating a sun space such as this can usher light into a dark entry or flood a dining

area with sunshine. A "Skywall" created by Lindal Sunrooms, which usually consists of a string of windows topped by a row of skylights inset several feet into the existing roof pitch, is another way to bring in light and views.

A WORD ABOUT GLASS

The difference between a truly year-round room and one that will fail you in extreme weather is the glass. Ordinary window glass won't do. You'll need energy-efficient, super-insulated glazing that protects you from sweltering in summer and shivering in winter. "Otherwise," says Jim Ruppel, "you might as well just build a porch."

Talk to your sunroom contractor about glazing options. The industry standard is double-pane glass, with an insulating dead-air space between the panes, that transmits

about 85 percent of visible available light. But for climates that experience weather extremes, high-performance glass, of which there are several types, would be a better choice. You'll pay a premium, but it will be well worth it in terms of the comfort and usability of your sunroom.

For more information on glazing options, or to find a sunroom dealer near you, contact the National Sunroom Association at (913) 266-7014. ■

ABOVE, LEFT TO RIGHT: Additions and renovated spaces are the ideal canvas for bold strokes of design, and light is one of the architect's best tools. Talk to your professionals about your hopes and dreams for your new space, and make sure they understand the world of options available from today's sunroom manufacturers. Then, let the interplay of shadow and sun, dark and light lead the way.

COZY KITCHENS

*Make the most of your smallish kitchen
with some clever planning and a direct link to the outdoors*

WRITTEN BY SARA BLISS

Before you hammer that first nail, consider your exteriors. Outdoor spaces are about joy. Whether you are enjoying a summertime backyard soiree, having a quiet dinner for two, or reading a novel in the sun, the spaces outside your home are perfect for relaxation, socializing, and dining. But, chances are, you spend the majority of your at-home time in the kitchen. So, how can you link the two spaces together; how can you bring the outdoors in and take the indoors out? As you plan your new house, knock down that boundary between the kitchen and the backyard. Here, we show you two kitchens that are completely connected to the outdoors.

ABOVE: It's important to make your outdoor room as comfortable and as enticing as your indoor spaces. The two patios shown here are inviting, and are both just steps away from the kitchen.

ABOVE LEFT: A hanging pot rack helps stretch storage space. The oversized windows make the smallish kitchen appear larger. **ABOVE RIGHT:** A glass door leading directly to the sunny patio connects the cook to the outdoors.

Take cues from these clever projects for combining contrasting styles, maximizing small spaces, bringing the outdoors in, and designing an alluring outdoor room.

OPPOSITES ATTRACT

When designing a totally new kitchen, don't match all the materials and styles in predictable ways. Instead, create a room that is completely your own by throwing in a visual surprise or two. Combine contrasting styles and materials—old with new, bold with feminine, or sleek with soft—to create an eye-catching room. Then, do the same for the outdoor space so there's a seamless flow from inside to out.

With the patio just steps off the kitchen, backyard soirees are a snap

MAXIMIZING A SMALL SPACE

Since the kitchen is often the heart of the home, it can be challenging when it is a small space. And that is why connecting it to the outdoors is so vital—it stretches your living space beyond the four walls. Of course, there are many things you can do to maximize a cramped kitchen inside the house. Clever storage is essential. Use open shelving and cabinets for storing more attractive items, such as books, serving plates, decorative trays, bowls, and baskets. Let closed cabinets and drawers hide food, cutlery, and anything you need but don't want on display. A hanging pot rack and a wine rack are also terrific space-savers that provide easy access to items. To add counter space, you can bring in a rolling work island for minimal expense. To make a small space appear bigger, Boston contractor Brian Vogt suggests painting the room a light color, adding as many doors and windows as possible, and using mirrors. Keep walls to a minimum. The open space will enable you to speak with guests and family as

French doors connect
to the covered porch,
bringing plenty of
sunlight indoors.

*Extra windows
let sunlight stream in
and provide a terrific
spot for staring
up at the stars*

you prepare food. And, French doors to the terrace or porch will offer you that connection to the outdoors even when you're stuck inside doing dishes.

BRING THE OUTDOORS IN

When envisioning your dream kitchen, look beyond the walls. Literally. Bring in the outdoors by adding rows of windows and glass doors. Not only will you let in more light and create an open, airy feeling even in a small kitchen, but you will also take advantage of the views, whether it's rows of trees, a mountain vista, or your own terrace. According to Vogt, another idea for connecting the indoors to the outdoors is to use materials inside that you normally see outdoors, such as slate, brick, or stone.

OUTDOOR DECOR

Design outdoor spaces as cozy and beautiful as your favorite indoor rooms. If you have a covered porch, you have more options for decorating than if you have an open area, because you don't have to worry about rain and weatherproof materials. But don't let that limit you; there are plenty of fabric and furniture lines that can hold up in harsh sun and drizzling rain; just do your homework. The main consideration: comfort. Outdoor rooms are about enjoyment and relaxation, so make them inviting. Provide lots of seating for extra guests, plenty of pillows and throws for lounging, and several tables for drinks, books, and snacks. ■

TOP: A sleek stainless-steel table shares space with a vintage white wood buffet. **BOTTOM:** A colorful rug, cozy wicker chairs, and a collection of pillows make the porch—right off the kitchen—the perfect room for entertaining.

BEYOND BARBECUING

*Start entertaining alfresco
by creating an outdoor 'kitchen'*

Nothing tops the outdoors for intensifying appetites and enhancing entertaining. And because we crave connection with the wide-open spaces, one of today's freshest home trends focuses on the outdoor kitchen. With the many innovative products available, your outdoor prep area can become sophisticated enough to help you create elegant gourmet feasts—as well as those tried-and-true grilled dinners.

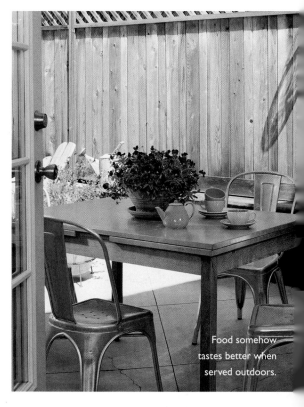

Food somehow tastes better when served outdoors.

WHERE TO BEGIN

When planning an outdoor kitchen, consider available area and good placement. The size of the kitchen will be determined by how much you want to include and how elaborate it will be—anywhere from a 5-by-5-foot corner to a 20-by-20-foot culinary center. For convenience, position it just beyond the indoor kitchen or family room. Provide a natural transition from indoors to outdoors with a large sliding door or multiple French doors. An existing deck or patio can work as a foundation, if you decide it's large enough, but decks may require additional support to accommodate heavy appliances and cabinetry. Choose weatherproof materials for cabinetry, countertops, sink, and exposed fixtures. Slate, teak, stainless steel, and stone are clearly good options.

If you decide a small built-in grill and storage cabinet will suffice, you may be able to install them yourself. However, if you're going all-out, seek the advice of a qualified professional—such as a Certified Kitchen Designer—and rely on licensed contractors

for installation of electrical and gas connections. For safety, insist on GFI (ground fault interrupters) for all electrical runs.

WHAT TO INCLUDE

The range of products available for outdoor kitchens is nearly as varied as that for indoor kitchens. Begin with the best grill you can afford, as this is the centerpiece of any outdoor kitchen. You'll find both free-standing and built-in models in gas, charcoal, and electric (for flame-restricted areas). Some grills even offer the flexibility of switching from gas to charcoal.

Features for grills include side burners, griddles, woks, and motorized rotisseries. Moveable grilling grids that can be adjusted to different heights are a convenient option. Or choose a grill with a built-in wood-chip tray for a true smoky flavor for meats and vegetables. Expect to pay anywhere from a few hundred dollars for a simple portable unit to $4,000 and up for an elaborate built-in model. Price will depend on the size of the grilling surface and number of BTUs (if gas) of the unit.

Refrigerators for outdoor kitchens are usually smaller under-counter varieties. For safety and easy maintenance they are fashioned of stainless steel with a water-resistant thermostat, sealed electrical contacts, and insulated electrical terminals. The most popular models are priced from $300 to $500.

If you're planning to make a real splash with your outdoor kitchen, consider special extras designed specifically to withstand the rigors of the outdoors:

- a small dishwasher set in a drawer
- a draft hood over the grill and side burners
- outlets for cable TV and a phone
- wine and beer coolers or a beverage center
- a fireplace or gas patio heater for cooler weather
- a warming drawer
- an icemaker
- a trash compactor.

Of course, you'll also want comfortable furniture and enough table space to accommodate dinner guests. Remember, whatever elements you choose, you're sure to have plenty of great dining experiences. ■

1 HOUSE, 101 IDEAS

Let this stunning and well-designed interior give you guidance while you plan for your new home

WRITTEN BY DIANE COURTNEY

As anyone who has ever planned a remodeling project can tell you, many of your best ideas will come from other houses—and some houses offer more inspiration than others. This house, a recently built getaway in eastern Long Island, takes an innovative path to a result we can all appreciate: average-size rooms that live large. It's a good lesson for all of us dedicated remodelers: Visiting model homes and showhouses is one of the smartest ways to get an inside look at the latest in design and materials. Or, you can study the following pages for 101 ways to help you remodel or redecorate.

ABOVE: Bold design and a great site are just the tip of the iceberg with this lovely home.

LIVING ROOM

1 Sky-high glazing.

2 A well-centered conversation area. The glass cocktail table acts as a focal point, drawing carefully placed seating in for an intimate effect.

3 A strong, simple hearth.

4 Clever contrast. Here, a light area rug stands out against the dark floor.

5 Windows that open out.

6 A visual anchor. The dark fireplace surround and the chairs in front of it anchor the room amidst sky's-the-limit views.

7 A quiet color palette.

8 Personal proportion. Placing the painting low on the mantel helps bring the eye down to conversation level—creating warmth despite the walls of glass.

9 A variety of textures. The soft, cushy sofa plays in subtle counterpoint to the angular elements surrounding it, lending an effect of casual comfort. The light upholstery reinforces the airy effect.

10 Invisible walls. The open plan provides a sense of flow, but well-placed furnishings clearly define different areas.

11 Judicious bursts of color. Even the most neutral room needs a little color—and bringing in even the tiniest bit can do a big job. And keep in mind that in an open plan several rooms can be seen at once—so color schemes and accents should be complementary.

12 A mix of hard and soft furnishings.

DINING ROOM

13 Pendants to add punch.

14 Juxtaposition. For extra impact, consider contrast, like these silvery aluminum chairs that appear to float against the dark

table and wood floors.

15 The right table. Using a narrow table long enough to seat ten comfortably allows for plenty of room to roam between the table and the wall. This ploy makes a limited dining space seem completely unconfined.

16 A sleek setting. The simple black sawhorse table echoes the dark flooring and provides a sleek, uncluttered background for table settings and food.

17 Plenty of ambient lighting.

18 Unexpected bursts of color. Tangerine makes for a pleasant surprise in the ceiling lights and plays up the citrus theme of the table setting.

19 Artwork that takes center stage.

20 Mixed motifs. Traditional wood candle holders contrast brilliantly with the contemporary white centerpiece, with a successfully eclectic effect.

21 Seating for a crowd.

22 Strong architecture. To achieve continuity of line, design, and color, the architecture of the room's outer wall of doors and windows continues in the lines of the beams and insets along the inside wall. The details work hard, too. For instance, the door hardware brings black back into play.

23 Glass accents.

FAMILY ROOM

24 Structural elements that make a design statement.

25 Perfect placement. Cleverly arranging furniture into a clearly separate grouping gives the house a family-friendly space—even though a wall of floor-to-ceiling windows

{36

{39

{38

41}

45}

46}

43}

continues from the living room into this "room."

26 A console with a strong role. Standing behind the living room sofa, the console table draws a definite line of demarcation between the living room and family area—and provides the perfect surface for a pair of table lamps.

27 Tonal variation. The two-tone design of the table eases the transition between rooms; the light wood on top of the dark table relates to the wood of the coffee table in the family room, preventing any hint of abruptness.

28 An emphasis on great views.

29 Outdoor style inside.

30 A put-your-feet-up approach. Plump cushioning is a necessity for getting good and comfortable in an area meant for relaxing. And the informal upholstery fabric, rough texture, and solid construction of the armchairs also contribute to the urge to lounge around.

31 A light hand with accessories. A few well-chosen decorations and a couple of books say, "Sit down and stay awhile"—without overpowering the space.

32 Gentle curves.

33 Endless horizons. Wrapping glazing around a corner creates the illusion of a space with new boundaries, making it feel bigger. Corner windows provide a wider view of the out-of-doors to boot; in this case, a tranquil view of the lawn rolling down to a bay.

34 Floor-to-ceiling glass. Extending windows low to the floor keeps you connected to the view while you're seated.

35 An area rug for definition.

KITCHEN AND BREAKFAST AREA

36 A distinctive chandelier.

37 The right mix of materials. Combining warm and cold surfaces is a good way to design a sharp contemporary edge into a room where you also want a warm, gather-round atmosphere.

38 Easy-open casement windows.

39 A fresh floral centerpiece.

40 A cohesive design philosophy. Repeated elements—like the dark flooring and countertops—keep this kitchen in perfect harmony with the rest of the house. Keep in mind that in an open-plan home like this one, flowing spaces are made even more effective by keeping the flow going in design and decoration. Adopting this strategy will

ensure that there are no disconcerting jolts as you move from room to room or see into one from another.

41 Retro furniture—for a completely contemporary look.

42 A focal point. The light-colored center island brightens the work area; the stainless-steel legs refer back to the breakfast table and chairs.

43 Minimalist stone floor tiles.

44 Glass doors. Clear glass cupboard doors

turn a corner for a continuous open look and provide a spot for showing off dishes and glassware.

45 Sleek seating.

46 Space-saving built-ins.

47 Double duty. A pair of tall pull-out faucets adds convenience to the prep and cleanup area—a welcome amenity in a two-cook kitchen.

48 Ceiling-high storage.

49 An oversized stone sink.

50 A moveable central island.

51 Windows to the world. Wrap-around windows make the breakfast nook seem huge. The open-and-airy effect makes the kitchen the nerve center of family life it should be—the perfect spot to chat with guests while making dinner, or just to linger over morning coffee while gazing out.

52 An extra-quiet dishwasher.

BEDROOM

53 Light-filtering window treatments.

54 Graphic design motifs.

55 Clutter-catchers. Bedside tables with large surfaces are essential—otherwise, you'll have no place to put books, eyeglasses, water, pencil and paper, the TV guide, and the remote control.

56 A good reading lamp.

57 A supportive headboard. Choose a bed designed for leaning; a pillow propped against this tall webbed headboard will offer plenty of support for reading or watching television in bed.

58 Natural beauty. Pamper yourself with fresh flowers every week.

59 Delicate accents to balance contemporary elements.

60 Softness underfoot. Carpeting that covers most of the floor area adds luxury to the entire room. Not only is it more comfortable to the feet, but it can relieve the starkness of contemporary furnishings, making the space more inviting.

61 Simplicity. Keeping decorative accessories to a minimum ensures an uncluttered, peaceful look. In this room, the only extemporaneous items allowed are the candles and flowers, which, in fact, add to the peaceful ambiance.

62 Luxurious—but understated—bedding.

63 Architectural interest. White-painted wainscoting on the walls adds an element of texture while maintaining the room's prevailing simplicity.

64 Storage near the bed.

MASTER BATH

65 Unexpected industrial touches.

66 A room-expanding mirror.

67 A vanity with space for two.

68 Clever use of light and reflection. The placement of the window—where it is reflected in the mirror—doubles the effect of light and space.

69 Storage for all the essentials. Plenty of

doors and drawers keep grooming paraphernalia out of sight.

70 Simple wood cabinetry.

71 Old fittings in a modern space.

72 Repeated materials. The dark stone vanity surface recalls the kitchen countertops and the dark wood tones used throughout the house—and provides a dramatic spot to show off a pretty potted plant.

73 Interesting architecture.

74 Extra storage under the eaves.

75 Sandy stone tiles.

76 Everyday elegance. Artfully arranged on the overhead shelves—and interspersed with a few decorative items—utilitarian items like towels become part of the design scheme.

77 A mix of materials. Combining shiny, matte, and wood-grained elements brings interest to the room without overwhelming the small space. Plenty of white adds a fresh, crisp look to the earth-toned

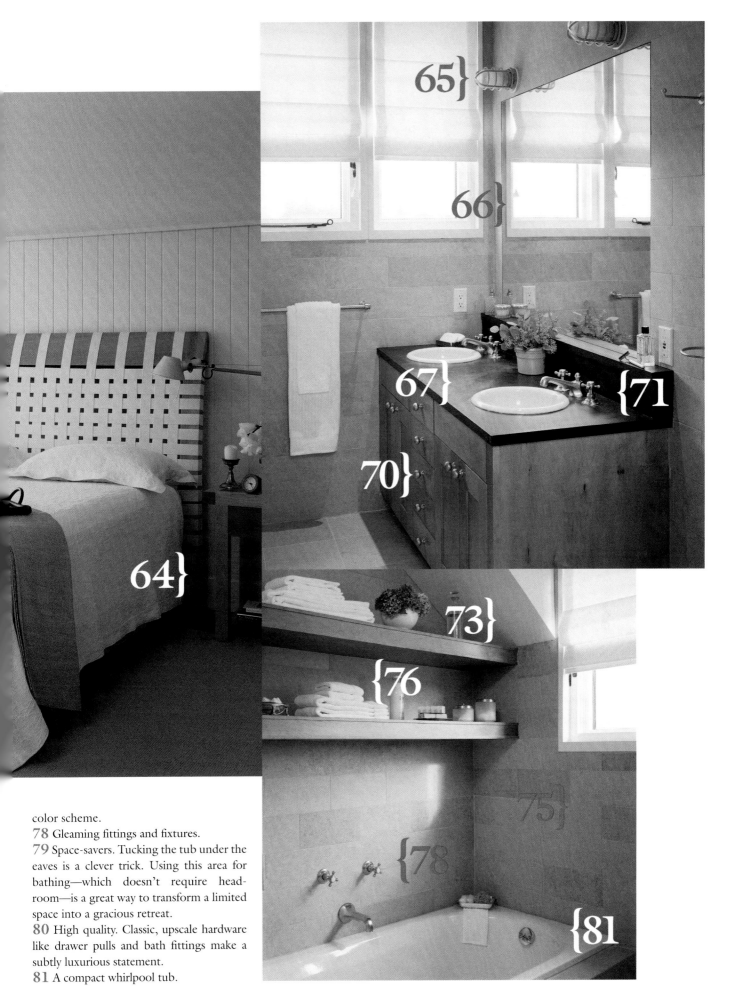

65}

66}

67}

{71

70}

64}

73}

{76

{75}

{78

{81

color scheme.

78 Gleaming fittings and fixtures.

79 Space-savers. Tucking the tub under the eaves is a clever trick. Using this area for bathing—which doesn't require head-room—is a great way to transform a limited space into a gracious retreat.

80 High quality. Classic, upscale hardware like drawer pulls and bath fittings make a subtly luxurious statement.

81 A compact whirlpool tub.

EXTERIOR

82 Intersecting geometric planes.

83 Natural-looking wood shingles.

84 Split personalities. The back of a house can open its arms to the joys of the outdoors, while the front of the house presents a face of sheltered privacy with modest, carefully placed windows and an inset entryway.

85 Never-ending glazing.

86 Room to relax.

87 Appropriate materials. The shingled façade fits the waterfront landscape and the shape of the house, and complements the shingled roof. Wood shakes also have the advantage of weathering naturally over time.

88 Gracious entertaining areas.

89 An interesting facade.

90 An inviting entry.

91 Separate, linked structures.

92 A beautiful garage door.

93 A shapely driveway. A driveway that sweeps up to the house in a pleasant curve contrasts nicely with the squared-off shapes of the building itself.

94 Well-proportioned landscaping.

95 Eye-catching arches.

96 Smart positioning. Convenient access to indoor food-preparation areas makes serving outdoor meals a pleasure.

97 Small steps. Gradual step-downs from outdoor eating areas to the patio provide easy indoor/outdoor transitions, helping the house relate to its site.

98 A strong connection between indoors and out.

99 An intimate breakfast spot.

100 Elegant furnishings. Decorate outdoor living spaces with as much care as you would your living room. Here, patio furniture is simple, handsome, and chosen to enhance its surroundings.

101 Multiple levels for extra interest. ■

DIVE IN

Everybody into the pool—the water's fine!

Maybe you've coveted a pool since childhood, when your next-door neighbors spent all summer splashing (loudly) in their state-of-the-art kidney-shaped oasis. Or maybe it's your wife, the exercise buff, who wants a convenient place to swim laps. Or your husband, the master gardener, who sees a pool as a natural extension of his carefully-honed landscape plan. Whatever (or whoever) your reason for investing in a pool, you'll find that your options are as varied as your imagination. So jump right in!

The right lighting can make your pool area an
extension of your home. Fiber-optic lighting
inside the pool lends a soft glow to the water;
attractive outdoor fixtures will illuminate
conversation nooks around the patio.

A dramatic setting demands a creative approach to pool planning. Here, a "disappearing edge" treatment gives the impression that the pool falls over the edge of the cliff.

A well-designed pool will be the jewel in the crown of your landscaping plan

Your pool can be so much more than just a hole filled with water—all it takes is a little planning and creativity on your part. Start by looking around your yard and deciding what the focus of the pool should be. Will you primarily use it for swimming laps, or do you hope to entertain large groups around its shimmering edges? And what's your budget? In-ground pools offer the greatest design versatility, but they range in price from $17,000 to $45,000 and up. Above-ground pools may cost as little as $1,500 to $5,000.

AN ARTISTIC APPROACH

If you'd like your pool to reflect your individual aesthetic, you're in luck. Today's design trends are wide and varied:

■ Murals are colorful complements to any pool design. Usually they are added to the walls or floor of a pool and can be created in mosaic tile, printed, or painted on.

■ Statues and columns add a refined, elegant touch. Large urns may serve as planters or fountains in and around the pool.

Once upon a time, when it came to pool design you had two choices: rectangular or kidney shaped. But these shapes suit few landscapes perfectly. Today's options, including pond or beach-like pool designs and elegant, classical edge treatments, allow homeowners to match their pool to the landscape that will surround it.

Choose your pool's shape with your home's architecture and its landscape in mind

As in interior design, shape and color are key to poolside style. Here, the pool's undulating lines and pale liner provide soft counterpoint to the traditional architecture of the house.

■ The infinity edge is sometimes called the "vanishing" edge or the "negative" edge. First developed in Europe, the infinity edge technique gives the illusion that the pool's edge disappears into thin air. Actually, a basin built below the edge catches the spilling water and recycles it back into the pool.

■ Fiber-optic lighting systems create a romantic ambiance but are easy to install and maintain. Perimeter lighting outlines the pool, spa, or other walkway, while a rotating color wheel turns water a rainbow of fantasy colors.

"NATURAL" BEAUTY

To help your pool blend into its surroundings, consider design elements inspired by nature:

■ Water features are among the most affordable amenities that can be added to your pool. Among the many variations are such choices as a cascading waterfall, a splashing fountain, or a meandering waterway.

■ Rock formations are usually constructed from a high-tech blend of polyurethane molding, so they're lightweight and easy to install.

■ Pebble technology provides tumbled pebbles and cement combined with water and additives to form a unique pool finish. This technology is also used to contour shoreline-like edges and sloping beach entries.

LEFT: Here, a dark-colored liner lends drama to a linear design approach. **TOP:** Divided into different areas for different uses, this pool is in essence a series of aquatic "rooms." **ABOVE:** Water features are a sure-fire way to make your pool a showstopper.

■ Misting systems are easy to install and affordable. They create a gentle fog over the pool and surrounding patio area, creating a dramatic effect and helping to keep the patio cooler. At night, the mist is particularly striking when used with the pool's water and lighting features.

PRACTICAL MATTERS

If you're worried you'll spend more time cleaning your pool than actually swimming in it, take heart: Advances in technology have made maintenance easy and automatic. Recent offerings include:

■ Aquatic computers that allow push-button maintenance of the pools' heater, filtration, and cleaning systems. Some systems can even be triggered from a remote location by a cell phone.

■ Super-efficient vacuuming systems for truly hands-off cleaning. Some vacuums scrub away unattended on the pool's floor, while others float above.

■ Automatic cleaning systems built into the pool for silent, invisible cleaning and circulation of water.

■ Natural water clarifiers developed from crab shells. They cause dirt, minerals, and oil to clump together for better filtration.

■ Saltwater, bromine, and mineral water purifiers. Some attach to pool vacuum hoses, while others are dropped right into the pool. ■

HEIGHTENED ELEGANCE

*This spacious, comfortable plan boasts a
rustic Craftsman appeal*

©1998 DONALD A. GARDNER, INC.,
PHOTOGRAPHY COURTESY OF DONALD A. GARDNER ARCHITECTS, INC.

The outdoors is never more than a few steps away thanks to the porches and covered patios that adorn this beautiful retreat. Inside, you'll enjoy modern comforts with an appeal to classic, rustic sensibilities. The great room occupies a central location, and rightly so. Branching off to one side are the cooking and dining areas, which are complemented by a screened porch with its own fireplace.

ABOVE: The angled wings draw guests into the arched entryway.

The stone fireplace strikes a commanding presence in the great room, which features a vaulted ceiling with exposed wood beams.

The kitchen boasts ample cooking and storage space, with a snack bar counter and a butler's pantry on the way towards the laundry room and garage. Down the stairs from the great room, you'll find a perfect place for a media or recreation room, complete with a hearth and a wet bar. Two bedrooms downstairs each enjoy private baths.

Back on the main level, the master suite begins with a private study or sitting room, featuring yet another fireplace. The suite continues to a private porch, large walk-in closet, and sumptuous bedrom situated to enjoy fantastic views. Two more bedrooms share a full bath in a wing of their own to the right of the entryway. ■

RIGHT: This luxurious bedroom enjoys panoramic views, arched windows, a soaring ceiling, and a spacious design.
BELOW: The great room's sitting area offers spectacular views of the backyard.

Enjoy private views
through the windows in
the luxurious master bath.

ptan# HPT9700001

STYLE: CRAFTSMAN
MAIN LEVEL: 3,040 SQ. FT.
LOWER LEVEL: 1,736 SQ. FT.
TOTAL: 4,776 SQ. FT.
BEDROOMS: 5
BATHROOMS: 4½
WIDTH: 106' - 5"
DEPTH: 104' - 2"

SEARCH ONLINE @ EPLANS.COM

MAIN LEVEL

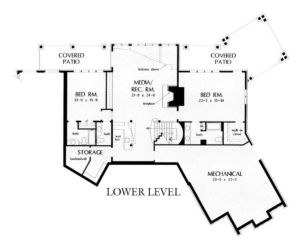

LOWER LEVEL

THE NOT-SO-HUMBLE ABODE

Twin turrets and a romantic balcony enhance the facade of this stunning chateau

EXTERIOR PHOTOGRAPHY BY VANTAGE POINT PHOTOGRAPHY, INC., INTERIOR PHOTOGRAPHY BY EVERETT & SOULE

This enchanting home, reminiscent of a castle with its two turrets and Chateau details, allows homeowners to live a true life of luxury. A raised vestibule, which leads to a grand circular foyer, provides an elegant introduction to the splendid floor plan. The dining room and library, each housed in a turret, both include fireplaces; the library also boasts a coffered ceiling. A central reception hall, perfect for formal entertaining, overlooks the rear veranda and pool. Nearby, the family gathering hall adjoins the gourmet kitchen, where a vast array of amenities—lots of counter space, a walk-in pantry, easy access to an outdoor herb garden, and enough space for two refrigerators—will please any cook.

ABOVE: Elegant landscaping, including a fountain, complements this castle-like dwelling perfectly.

plan# HPT9700002

STYLE: FRENCH
FIRST FLOOR: 3,874 SQ. FT.
SECOND FLOOR: 2,588 SQ. FT.
TOTAL: 6,462 SQ. FT.
BEDROOMS: 4
BATHROOMS: 5½ + ½
WIDTH: 146' - 8"
DEPTH: 84' - 4"
FOUNDATION: SLAB

SEARCH ONLINE @ EPLANS.COM

The master suite, to the left of the plan, provides the latest luxuries as well, with His and Hers wardrobes and a grand private bath that features a step-up tub, a walk-in shower, and access to a private garden.

Upstairs, the comfort continues, with three bedrooms all featuring private baths and walk-in closets. A spacious media room, with a balcony that overlooks the family gathering hall, can serve as a home theater, and the billiards/game area opens to the upper terrace. ■

ABOVE: The fireplace serves as a focal point of the family gathering hall.

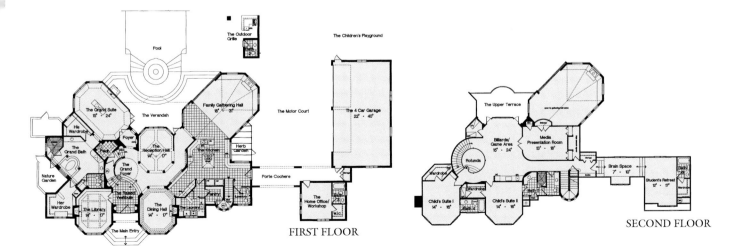

FIRST FLOOR

SECOND FLOOR

EUROPEAN MANOR

*Bring the French countryside home with
this magnificent estate*

PHOTOGRAPHY BY ANDREW D. LAUTMAN

The distinctive covered entry to this stunning Norman manor, flanked by twin turrets, leads to a gracious foyer. The foyer opens to a formal dining room, a study, and a step-down gathering room. The study offers a built-in desk, and special features in the gathering room include a wet bar, easy access to the rear terrace, and a large raised hearth flanked by two art niches. The spacious kitchen also boasts numerous amenities, including an island workstation and a built-in desk. The adjacent morning room opens to the terrace. The secluded master suite offers two walk-in closets, a dressing area, a bath with a whirlpool tub that overlooks a side courtyard, and an exercise area with a built-in spa. The second floor features four bedrooms—one with a walk-in closet—and an oversized activities room with a raised-hearth fireplace and access to a balcony.

ABOVE: Twin turrets and heavy wooden doors establish this plan's Norman influences.

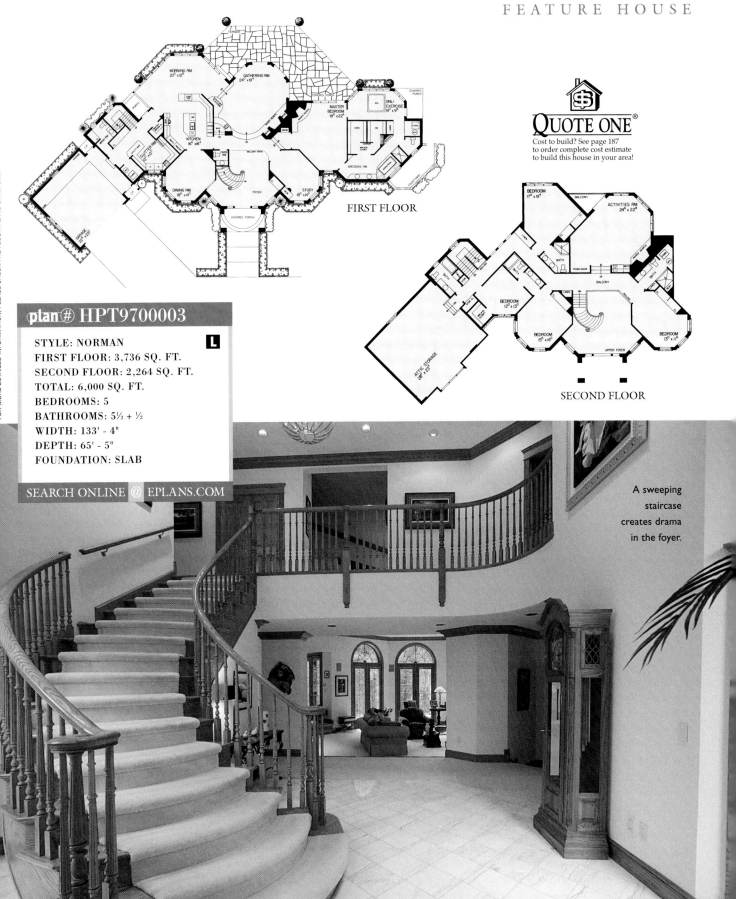

FIRST FLOOR

SECOND FLOOR

Quote One®
Cost to build? See page 187
to order complete cost estimate
to build this house in your area!

plan# HPT9700003 L

STYLE: NORMAN
FIRST FLOOR: 3,736 SQ. FT.
SECOND FLOOR: 2,264 SQ. FT.
TOTAL: 6,000 SQ. FT.
BEDROOMS: 5
BATHROOMS: 5½ + ½
WIDTH: 133' - 4"
DEPTH: 65' - 5"
FOUNDATION: SLAB

SEARCH ONLINE @ EPLANS.COM

A sweeping
staircase
creates drama
in the foyer.

MEDITERRANEAN OASIS

Window walls in every room open this plan to the outdoors

PHOTOGRAPHY BY OSCAR THOMPSON

Luxurious dreams and contemporary style combine to give this home striking appeal. A stunning courtyard entry welcomes you inside. Two guest suites with pampering private baths flank the foyer. A bridge leads over the pool to an outdoor kitchen enhanced by skylights. The gathering room features an impressive bar. The left wing of the home offers a gourmet kitchen, which is open to the leisure room and nook—the dining room connects close by. Stairs lead up to a bonus room with a private deck. The left wing of the home is devoted to the master suite, which features steps up to a private sitting retreat. Double doors lead into a lavish master bath that boasts an impressive bath, separate shower, twin vanities, a compartmented toilet, and His and Hers walk-in closets. Private access to the study is a convenient touch. An extensive wraparound deck surrounds the pool.

ABOVE: A soaring portico creates a striking entry for this plan. **RIGHT:** Dramatic lighting enhances the deck and pool area.

plan# HPT9700004

STYLE: MEDITERRANEAN
SQUARE FOOTAGE: 5,887
BONUS SPACE: 570 SQ. FT.
BEDROOMS: 3
BATHROOMS: 3½
WIDTH: 137' - 4"
DEPTH: 103' - 0"
FOUNDATION: BLOCK

SEARCH ONLINE @ EPLANS.COM

SECOND TO NONE

This stunning home is Shangri-la from the inside out

ALL IMAGES SUPPLIED BY: TERREBONE PHOTOGRAPHY

Keystone lintels over the windows create a formal look for this brick country home. The well-planned interior blends comfort and formality; guests and homeowners will enjoy the open rooms, wide views, and smart details. A two-story foyer with a barrel-vaulted ceiling creates a sense of spaciousness, and provides a fine introduction to the rest of the home's rich amenities. The center hall, which opens through French doors to the rear property, features a marble floor with limestone inlay. Formal rooms include a two-story library—with a fireplace and built-in bookshelves—and a spacious dining room with a dome ceiling and lovely triple window. A gourmet kitchen, accessible from the dining room through a butler's pantry, features a walk-in pantry, an angled double sink, and access to a private covered porch. Nearby, the vaulted family room includes a fireplace and opens to a covered side porch. The first-floor master suite boasts a two-story walk-in closet, as well as a vaulted bath with a spa-style tub and an oversized shower. Upstairs, two family bedrooms share a compartmented bath, and a third bedroom offers a private bath.

BELOW: With an impressive brick exterior, this plan offers timeless appeal. **RIGHT:** Set a classical stage in this gorgeous backyard, complete with a fountain and covered lanai.

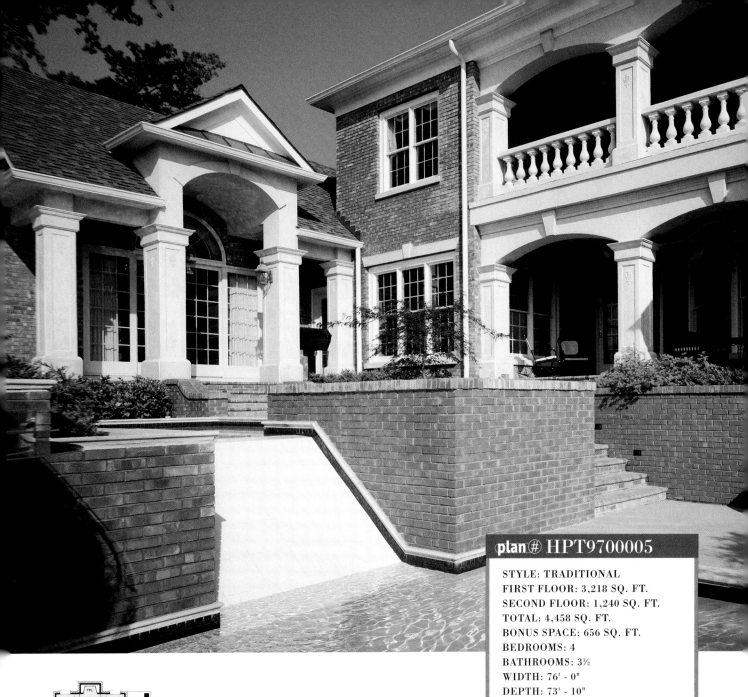

plan# HPT9700005

STYLE: TRADITIONAL
FIRST FLOOR: 3,218 SQ. FT.
SECOND FLOOR: 1,240 SQ. FT.
TOTAL: 4,458 SQ. FT.
BONUS SPACE: 656 SQ. FT.
BEDROOMS: 4
BATHROOMS: 3½
WIDTH: 76' - 0"
DEPTH: 73' - 10"
FOUNDATION: BASEMENT

SEARCH ONLINE @ EPLANS.COM

FIRST FLOOR

SECOND FLOOR

MELROSE PLANTATION

*The clean lines, welcoming porches, and soaring columns
of this home depict the very essence of the South*

PHOTOGRAPHY COURTESY OF: WILLIAM E. POOLE DESIGNS, INC.

This stately manor brings to mind the grandeur of a fading age. The pedimented, columned porch commands awe and acts as centerpiece to the perfectly symmetrical facade. Inside, formality reigns at the front of the plan, with an elegant dining room and formal living room flanking the large foyer. Ahead, past the staircase, find the gallery hall, which opens through double columns to the more casual family room. Here, a warming hearth and outdoor access will be enjoyed by family and guests. Another set of double columns on the left introduces the breakfast area and island kitchen. To the rear of these rooms, convenience is provided by a half-bath, mudroom, and utility area. A truly pampering master suite resides on the opposite side of the plan. Upstairs, three bedrooms each have a private bath. An exercise room, rec room, and office space complete the second floor.

ABOVE: This new home looks at first glance like it has been part of the landscape for decades.

The upstairs hallway provides tremendous views, both down to the foyer and outside through the second-floor porch.

plan# HPT9700006

STYLE: GREEK REVIVAL
FIRST FLOOR: 3,749 SQ. FT.
SECOND FLOOR: 1,631 SQ. FT.
TOTAL: 5,380 SQ. FT.
BONUS SPACE: 1,171 SQ. FT.
BEDROOMS: 4
BATHROOMS: 4½ + ½
WIDTH: 92' - 4"
DEPTH: 112' - 0"
FOUNDATION: CRAWLSPACE, BASEMENT

SEARCH ONLINE @ EPLANS.COM

FIRST FLOOR

SECOND FLOOR

DEFINING EXCELLENCE

Combining elegance and innovation, this Sun Country home is nothing short of delightful

PHOTOGRAPHY BY ©LAURENCE TAYLOR PHOTOGRAPHY

A unique courtyard provides a happy medium for indoor/outdoor living in this design. Inside, the foyer opens to a grand salon with a wall of glass, providing unobstructed views of the backyard. Informal areas include a leisure room with an entertainment center and glass doors that open to a covered poolside lanai. An outdoor fireplace enhances casual gatherings. The master suite is filled with amenities that include a bayed sitting area, access to the rear lanai, His and Hers closets, and a soaking tub. Upstairs, two family bedrooms—both with private decks—share a full bath. A detached guest house has a cabana bath and an outdoor grill area.

ABOVE: With nearly 3,500 square feet, this home offers ample space for a family of any size.

LEFT: Grand 14-foot windows illuminate interior spaces in the master suite.
BELOW: Elliptical windows and a two-story coffered ceiling highlight the grand salon.

The lanai offers a private oasis highlighted by a lagoon-style pool.

plan# HPT9700123

STYLE: FLORIDIAN
FIRST FLOOR: 2,853 SQ. FT.
SECOND FLOOR: 627 SQ. FT.
TOTAL: 3,480 SQ. FT.
BEDROOMS: 3
BATHROOMS: 2½
WIDTH: 80' - 0"
DEPTH: 96' - 0"
FOUNDATION: SLAB

SEARCH ONLINE @ EPLANS.COM

FIRST FLOOR

SECOND FLOOR

plan# HPT9700007

STYLE: ITALIANATE
FIRST FLOOR: 2,841 SQ. FT.
SECOND FLOOR: 1,052 SQ. FT.
TOTAL: 3,893 SQ. FT.
BEDROOMS: 4
BATHROOMS: 3½
WIDTH: 85' - 0"
DEPTH: 76' - 8"
FOUNDATION: CRAWLSPACE

SEARCH ONLINE @ EPLANS.COM

Ensure an elegant lifestyle with this luxurious plan. A turret, two-story bay windows, and plenty of arched glass impart a graceful style to the exterior, and rich amenities inside furnish contentment. A grand foyer decked with columns introduces the living room with curved-glass windows viewing the rear gardens. The study and living room share a through-fireplace. The master suite enjoys a tray ceiling, two walk-in closets, a separate shower, and a garden tub set in a bay window. Informal entertainment will be a breeze with a rich leisure room adjoining the kitchen and breakfast nook and opening to a rear veranda. Upstairs, two family bedrooms and a guest suite with a private deck complete the plan.

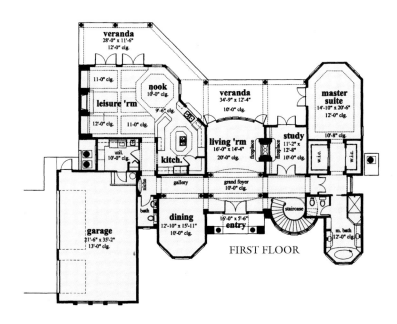

FIRST FLOOR

SECOND FLOOR

A hint of Moroccan architecture, with columns, arches, and walls of glass, makes an arresting appearance in this home. It allows a diverse arrangement of space inside, for a dynamic floor plan. The foyer spills openly into the immense living area and sunken dining room. A stair encircles the sunken library—a great space for a home theater. Beyond is the family room with a two-story high media wall and built-ins, plus the circular breakfast room and island kitchen. A maid's room, or guest room, has a full circular wall of glass and leads to the garage through a covered entry and drive-through area. The master suite is true luxury: circular sitting area, His and Hers facilities, and a private garden. Upstairs is a game room, plus two family bedrooms with private amenity-filled baths.

ptan# HPT9700008

STYLE: MEDITERRANEAN
FIRST FLOOR: 4,284 SQ. FT.
SECOND FLOOR: 1,319 SQ. FT.
TOTAL: 5,603 SQ. FT.
BEDROOMS: 4
BATHROOMS: 4½ + ½
WIDTH: 109' - 4"
DEPTH: 73' - 2"
FOUNDATION: SLAB

SEARCH ONLINE @ EPLANS.COM

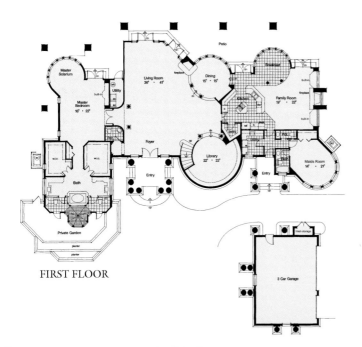

FIRST FLOOR

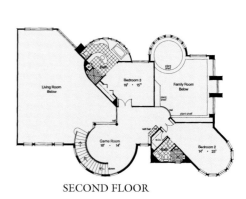

SECOND FLOOR

plan# HPT9700009

STYLE: CONTEMPORARY
FIRST FLOOR: 3,236 SQ. FT.
SECOND FLOOR: 494 SQ. FT.
TOTAL: 3,730 SQ. FT.
BEDROOMS: 4
BATHROOMS: 3½
WIDTH: 80' - 0"
DEPTH: 89' - 10"
FOUNDATION: SLAB

SEARCH ONLINE @ EPLANS.COM

If you want to build a home light years ahead of most other designs—nontraditional, yet addresses every need for your family—this showcase home is for you. From the moment you walk into this home, you are confronted with wonderful interior architecture that reflects modern, yet refined taste. The exterior says contemporary; the interior creates special excitement. Note the special rounded corners found throughout the home and the many amenities. The master suite is especially appealing with a fireplace and grand bath. Upstairs are a library/sitting room and a very private den or guest bedroom.

FIRST FLOOR

SECOND FLOOR

© HOME DESIGN SERVICES, INC.

This fresh and innovative design creates unbeatable ambiance. The breakfast nook and family room both open to a patio—a perfect arrangement for informal entertaining. The dining room is sure to please with elegant pillars separating it from the sunken living room. A media room delights both with its shape and by being convenient to the nearby kitchen—great for snack runs. A private garden surrounds the master bath and its spa tub and enormous walk-in closet. The master bedroom is enchanting with a fireplace and access to the outdoors. Additional family bedrooms come in a variety of different shapes and sizes; Bedroom 4 reigns over the second floor and features its own full bath.

plan# HPT9700010

STYLE: CONTEMPORARY
FIRST FLOOR: 3,770 SQ. FT.
SECOND FLOOR: 634 SQ. FT.
TOTAL: 4,404 SQ. FT.
BEDROOMS: 4
BATHROOMS: 3½
WIDTH: 87' - 0"
DEPTH: 97' - 6"
FOUNDATION: SLAB

SEARCH ONLINE @ EPLANS.COM

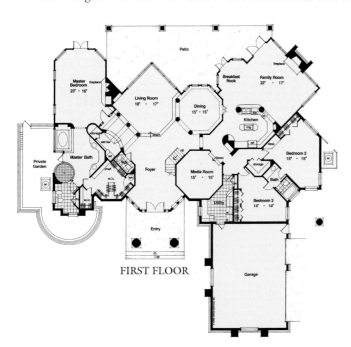

FIRST FLOOR

SECOND FLOOR

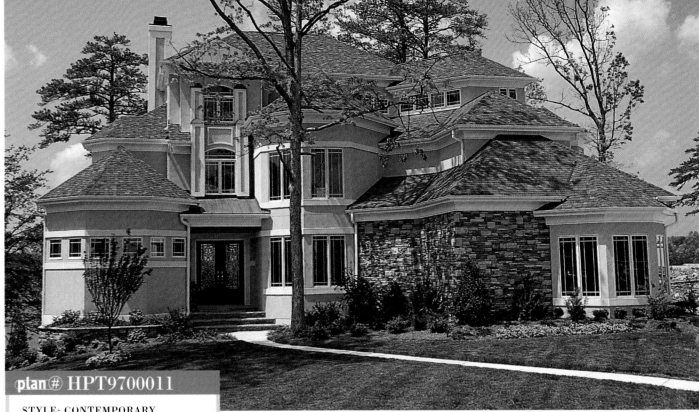

THIS HOME, AS SHOWN IN THE PHOTOGRAPH, MAY DIFFER FROM THE ACTUAL BLUEPRINTS. FOR MORE DETAILED INFORMATION, PLEASE CHECK THE FLOOR PLANS CAREFULLY.

plan # HPT9700011

STYLE: CONTEMPORARY
FIRST FLOOR: 2,347 SQ. FT.
SECOND FLOOR: 1,800 SQ. FT.
THIRD FLOOR: 1,182 SQ. FT.
TOTAL: 5,329 SQ. FT.
BASEMENT: 1,688 SQ. FT.
BEDROOMS: 4
BATHROOMS: 4½
WIDTH: 75' - 5"
DEPTH: 76' - 4"
FOUNDATION: BASEMENT

SEARCH ONLINE @ EPLANS.COM

A level for everyone! On the first floor, there's a study with a full bath, a formal dining room, a grand room with a fireplace, and a fabulous kitchen with an adjacent morning room. The second floor contains three suites—each with walk-in closets—two full baths, a loft, and a reading nook. A lavish master suite on the third floor is full of amenities, including His and Hers walk-in closets, a huge private bath, and a balcony. In the basement, casual entertaining takes off with a large gathering room, a home theater, and a spacious game room.

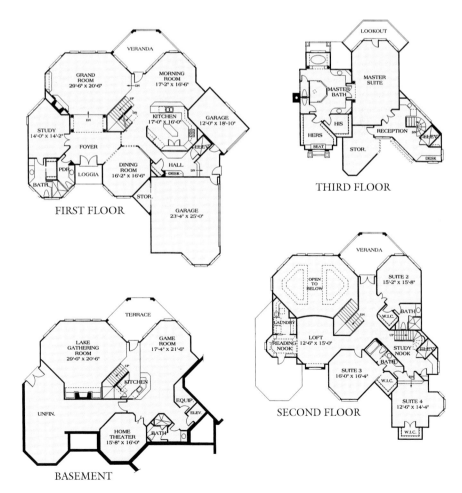

FIRST FLOOR

THIRD FLOOR

SECOND FLOOR

BASEMENT

© The Sater Design Collection, Inc.

Capturing the best of New England Colonial architecture, this stately brick manor includes appealing features, both classic and modern. Formal rooms toward the front are sure to impress, but the heart of the home is the kitchen and leisure room area. The country kitchen has an island and plenty of counter space to accommodate most any appliance. A bayed nook adds charm. The leisure room has a warming fireplace, built-in entertainment center, and sweeping rear views. Don't miss the built-in wine cellar, just outside the kitchen. Rear outdoor living areas include an open-air kitchen for exciting alfresco dining. The upper level includes three family suites (each with private baths and porch access) and a beautiful master retreat with a refreshing bath and soothing whirlpool tub.

plan# HPT9700012

STYLE: FRENCH
FIRST FLOOR: 2,163 SQ. FT.
SECOND FLOOR: 2,302 SQ. FT.
TOTAL: 4,465 SQ. FT.
BEDROOMS: 5
BATHROOMS: 5½
WIDTH: 58' - 0"
DEPTH: 65' - 0"
FOUNDATION: SLAB

SEARCH ONLINE @ EPLANS.COM

FIRST FLOOR

SECOND FLOOR

© The Sater Design Collection, Inc.

plan# HPT9700013

STYLE: ITALIANATE
FIRST FLOOR: 1,996 SQ. FT.
SECOND FLOOR: 2,171 SQ. FT.
TOTAL: 4,167 SQ. FT.
BEDROOMS: 5
BATHROOMS: 5½
WIDTH: 58' - 0"
DEPTH: 65' - 0"
FOUNDATION: SLAB

SEARCH ONLINE @ EPLANS.COM

Beautiful stone accents add warmth to this Italianate stucco home. Porches front and rear enhance the bright, airy sensation of natural light from expansive windows throughout. From the entry, the foyer opens to a living room/dining room combination, desired for its unlimited design potential. French doors to the right present a library/study with a two-way fireplace. In the kitchen, gourmet meals are a snap; abundant counter and cabinet space, an island, and room for professional-grade appliances will please the family chef. Between the kitchen and the comfortable leisure room, a nook could be a breakfast area or cozy reading spot. Upstairs, an angled master retreat lives up to its name, with lots of light, a fantastic spa bath and two enormous walk-in closets. Three more bedrooms include private baths—Bedroom 1 has a romantic balcony.

FIRST FLOOR

SECOND FLOOR

Reminiscent of a Mediterranean villa, this grand manor is a showstopper on the out-side and a comfortable residence on the inside. An elegant receiving hall boasts a double staircase and is flanked by the formal dining room and the library. A huge gathering room at the back is graced by a fireplace and a wall of sliding glass doors to the rear terrace. The master bedroom resides on the first floor for privacy. With a lavish bath to pamper you and His and Hers walk-in closets, this suite will be a delight to retire to each evening. Upstairs are four additional bedrooms with ample storage space, a large balcony overlooking the gathering room, and two full baths.

plan# HPT9700014

STYLE: MEDITERRANEAN
FIRST FLOOR: 3,350 SQ. FT.
SECOND FLOOR: 1,298 SQ. FT.
TOTAL: 4,648 SQ. FT.
BEDROOMS: 5
BATHROOMS: 3½ + ½
WIDTH: 97' - 0"
DEPTH: 74' - 4"
FOUNDATION: BASEMENT

SEARCH ONLINE @ EPLANS.COM

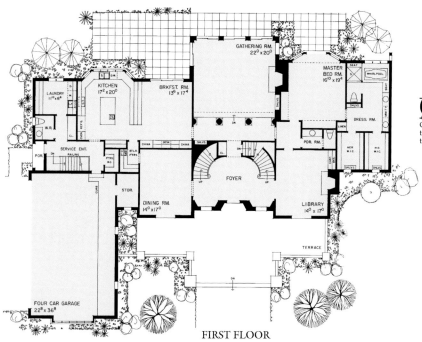

FIRST FLOOR

QUOTE ONE®

Cost to build? See page 187 to order complete cost estimate to build this house in your area!

SECOND FLOOR

plan# HPT9700015

STYLE: MEDITERRANEAN
FIRST FLOOR: 3,703 SQ. FT.
SECOND FLOOR: 1,427 SQ. FT.
TOTAL: 5,130 SQ. FT.
BONUS SPACE: 1,399 SQ. FT.
BEDROOMS: 4
BATHROOMS: 3½ + ½
WIDTH: 125' - 2"
DEPTH: 58' - 10"
FOUNDATION: WALKOUT
BASEMENT

SEARCH ONLINE @ EPLANS.COM

This magnificent estate is detailed with exterior charm: a porte cochere connecting the detached garage to the house, a covered terrace, and oval windows. The first floor consists of a lavish master suite, a cozy library with a fireplace, a grand room/solarium combination, and an elegant formal dining room with another fireplace. Three bedrooms dominate the second floor—each features a walk-in closet. For the kids, there is a playroom and, up another flight of stairs, is a room for future expansion into a deluxe studio with a fireplace. Over the three-car garage, there is space for a future mother-in-law or maid's suite.

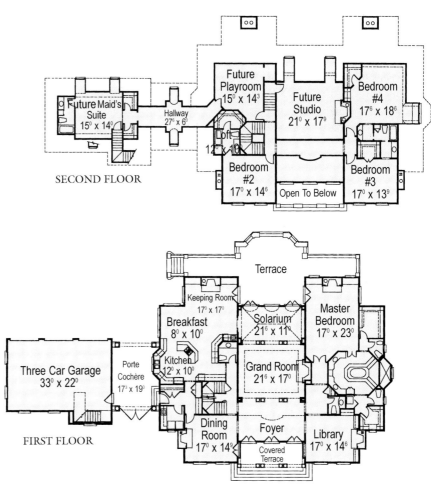

plan# HPT9700016

STYLE: FRENCH
FIRST FLOOR: 3,745 SQ. FT.
SECOND FLOOR: 1,643 SQ. FT.
TOTAL: 5,388 SQ. FT.
BONUS SPACE: 510 SQ. FT.
BEDROOMS: 5
BATHROOMS: 4½ + ½
WIDTH: 100' - 0"
DEPTH: 70' - 1"
FOUNDATION: SLAB, BASEMENT

SEARCH ONLINE @ EPLANS.COM

Steep rooflines and plenty of windows create a sophisticated aura around this home. Columns support the balconies above as well as the entry below. An angled family room featuring a fireplace is great for rest and relaxation. Snacks and sunlight are just around the corner with the nearby breakfast room and island kitchen. A ribbon of windows in the living room makes for an open feel. A bay-windowed study/library has two sets of French doors—one to the living room and one to the master suite. The master bedroom offers a bath with dual vanities and a spacious walk-in closet. Three family bedrooms are located on the upper level with a recreation/media room and an optional bonus room.

FIRST FLOOR

SECOND FLOOR

plan# HPT9700124

STYLE: FRENCH COUNTRY
FIRST FLOOR: 3,501 SQ. FT.
SECOND FLOOR: 2,582 SQ. FT.
TOTAL: 6,083 SQ. FT.
BEDROOMS: 6
BATHROOMS: 5½ + ½
WIDTH: 89' - 8"
DEPTH: 116' - 7"
FOUNDATION: BASEMENT

SEARCH ONLINE @ EPLANS.COM

The portico of this stunning European-style cottage offers a touch of whimsy to a stately facade. Inside, the foyer opens to a formal dining room and a quiet study. The grand room boasts a fireplace and leads outdoors to a covered lanai. A screened porch offers a private place for morning meals for the homeowner. The gourmet kitchen overlooks a spacious gathering room and shares the warmth of its fireplace, and a stunning sun room is accessible from the gathering room. Upstairs, four additional suites share a balcony hall. A recreation room leads to an upper hall and Suite 6, which offers accommodations to a guest or live-in relative.

FIRST FLOOR

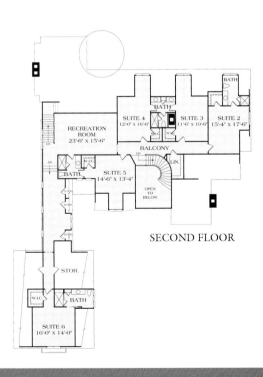

SECOND FLOOR

SECOND FLOOR

FIRST FLOOR

plan# HPT9700018

STYLE: FRENCH
FIRST FLOOR: 5,152 SQ. FT.
SECOND FLOOR: 726 SQ. FT.
TOTAL: 5,878 SQ. FT.
BEDROOMS: 4
BATHROOMS: 5½
WIDTH: 146' - 7"
DEPTH: 106' - 7"
FOUNDATION: SLAB

SEARCH ONLINE @ EPLANS.COM

Luxury abounds in this graceful manor. The formal living and dining rooms bid greeting as you enter and the impressive great room awaits more casual times with its cathedral ceiling and raised-hearth fireplace. A gallery hall leads to the kitchen and the family sleeping wing on the right and to the study, guest suite, and master suite on the left. The large island kitchen offers a sunny breakfast nook. The master suite includes a bayed sitting area, a dual fireplace shared with the study, and a luxurious bath. Each additional bedroom features its own bath and sitting area. Upstairs is a massive recreation room with a sunlit studio area and a bridge leading to an attic over the garage.

plan# HPT9700019

STYLE: COUNTRY COTTAGE
SQUARE FOOTAGE: 4,825
BEDROOMS: 4
BATHROOMS: 4½
WIDTH: 155' - 6"
DEPTH: 60' - 4"
FOUNDATION: SLAB

SEARCH ONLINE @ EPLANS.COM

In this English Country design, a series of hipped roofs cover an impressive brick facade accented by fine wood detailing. Formal living and dining rooms flank the foyer, while the nearby media room is designed for home theater and surround sound. Fireplaces warm the living room and the family room, which also boasts a cathedral ceiling. The kitchen offers plenty of work space, a bright breakfast nook, and access to two covered patios. Convenient to all areas of the house, the barrel-vaulted study has a wall of windows and French doors that can be closed for private meetings or quiet relaxing. All four bedrooms have private baths and walk-in closets. The master suite has the added luxury of a glass-enclosed sitting area.

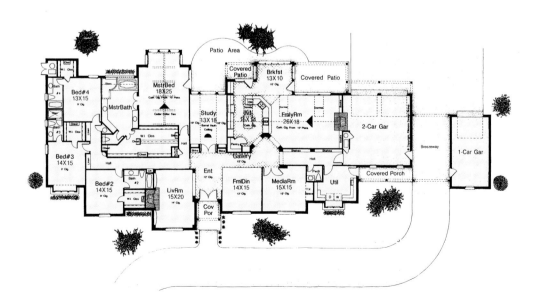

plan# HPT9700020

Elegance and luxury define this stately brick-and-stucco home. Creative design continues inside with a dramatic foyer that leads to the formal living and dining rooms and the casual two-story family room. A butler's pantry links the dining room to the grand kitchen. Casual gatherings will be enjoyed in the family room that joins with the breakfast room and kitchen. Here, a solarium and porch invite outdoor living. The exquisite master suite features a lush bath and sunny sitting area. Upstairs, two family bedrooms with private baths, a home office, and a hobby room round out the plan.

STYLE: TRADITIONAL
FIRST FLOOR: 3,065 SQ. FT.
SECOND FLOOR: 1,969 SQ. FT.
TOTAL: 5,034 SQ. FT.
BEDROOMS: 4
BATHROOMS: 3½
WIDTH: 88' - 6"
DEPTH: 45' - 0"
FOUNDATION: WALKOUT BASEMENT

SEARCH ONLINE @ EPLANS.COM

QUOTE ONE®
Cost to build? See page 187
to order complete cost estimate
to build this house in your area!

FIRST FLOOR

SECOND FLOOR

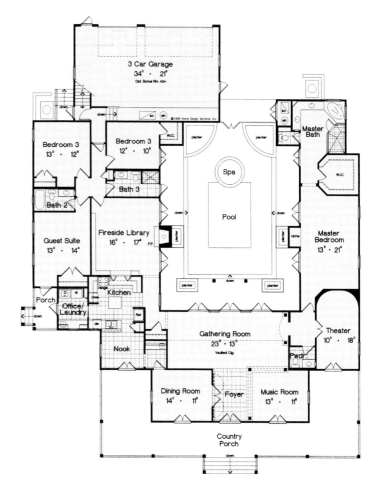

plan# HPT9700021

STYLE: FARMHOUSE
SQUARE FOOTAGE: 3,886
BEDROOMS: 4
BATHROOMS: 3½
WIDTH: 77' - 4"
DEPTH: 99' - 0"
FOUNDATION: SLAB

SEARCH ONLINE @ EPLANS.COM

Rustic elegance is the theme of this country marvel. An inviting country covered porch wraps around the front. To the right of the foyer, a quaint music room is open to the vaulted gathering room. The central splendor of this design is the family pool and indulging spa. To the right of the pool room, the master suite is secluded for privacy and includes a luxury-style master bath. Next to the master bedroom, a private theater is a quiet and relaxing retreat. A fireside library creates a romantic allure and is an appropriate addition to this heavenly plan.

© 1999 Donald A. Gardner, Inc.

This extraordinary four-bedroom estate features gables with decorative wood brackets, arched windows, and a stone-and-siding facade for undeniable Craftsman character. At the heart of the home, a magnificent cathedral ceiling adds space and stature to the impressive great room, which accesses both back porches. Sharing the great room's cathedral ceiling, a loft makes an excellent reading nook. Tray ceilings adorn the dining room and library/media room; all four bedrooms enjoy cathedral ceilings. A sizable kitchen is open to a large family room for ultimate togetherness. The master suite features back-porch access, a lavish private bath, and an oversized walk-in closet. A spacious bonus room is located over the three-car garage for further expansion. There are three additional family bedrooms—one easily converts to a study.

plan# HPT9700022

STYLE: CRAFTSMAN
FIRST FLOOR: 3,555 SQ. FT.
SECOND FLOOR: 250 SQ. FT.
TOTAL: 3,805 SQ. FT.
BONUS SPACE: 490 SQ. FT.
BEDROOMS: 4
BATHROOMS: 3
WIDTH: 99' - 8"
DEPTH: 78' - 8"

SEARCH ONLINE @ EPLANS.COM

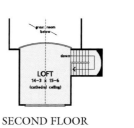

FIRST FLOOR

SECOND FLOOR

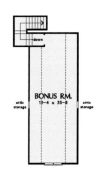

plan# HPT9700023

STYLE: TRADITIONAL
SQUARE FOOTAGE: 4,523
BEDROOMS: 4
BATHROOMS: 4½
WIDTH: 114' - 4"
DEPTH: 82' - 3"

SEARCH ONLINE @ EPLANS.COM

Large and rambling, this four-bedroom home is sure to please every member of the family. The homeowner will especially appreciate the master bedroom suite. Here, luxuries such as His and Hers bathrooms, two walk-in closets, and a tray ceiling await to pamper. For gatherings, the spacious great room lives up to its name, with a fireplace, built-ins, a tray ceiling, and access to the rear porch. The kitchen features an island cooktop/snack bar, a walk-in pantry, and an adjacent bayed breakfast room. A sunroom is also nearby. Note the storage in the three-car garage.

The stone and brick exterior with multiple gables and a side-entry garage creates a design that brags great curb appeal. The gourmet kitchen with an island and snack bar combines with the spacious breakfast room and hearth room to create a warm and friendly atmosphere for family living. The luxurious master bedroom with a sitting area and fireplace is complemented by a deluxe dressing room and walk-in closet. The basement level contains an office, media room, billiards room, exercise area and plenty of storage.

plan# HPT9700024

STYLE: TRADITIONAL
SQUARE FOOTAGE: 3,570
BASEMENT: 2,367 SQ. FT.
BEDROOMS: 3
BATHROOMS: 3½
WIDTH: 84' - 6"
DEPTH: 69' - 4"
FOUNDATION: BASEMENT

SEARCH ONLINE @ EPLANS.COM

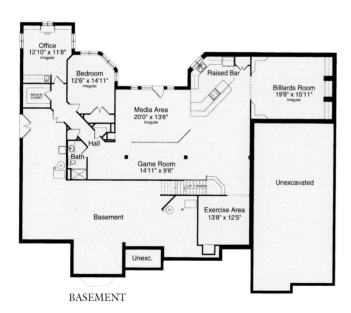

BASEMENT

FIRST FLOOR

plan# HPT9700025

STYLE: TRANSITIONAL
SQUARE FOOTAGE: 4,007
BASEMENT: 2,816 SQ. FT.
BEDROOMS: 2
BATHROOMS: 2½ + ½
WIDTH: 92' - 0"
DEPTH: 76' - 4"
FOUNDATION: BASEMENT

SEARCH ONLINE @ EPLANS.COM

This sprawling ranch-style home may have rustic charm, but this beautiful design is pure luxury. Stone accents frame a welcoming front porch; inside, raised ceilings begin with a formal foyer. Continue to the great room, graced with a warming fireplace and expansive rear views. An angled country kitchen easily serves the bright breakfast nook and formal dining room, defined by columns and adorned with French doors to the front porch. A cozy hearth room flows into a generous bedroom suite. The right wing comprises a stunning library and opulent master suite; here, a raised ceiling, fantastic bath, and His and Hers walk-in closets set the stage for decadence. On the lower level, two additional bedrooms share their space with a media room, wet bar, exercise room, billiards area, and game room.

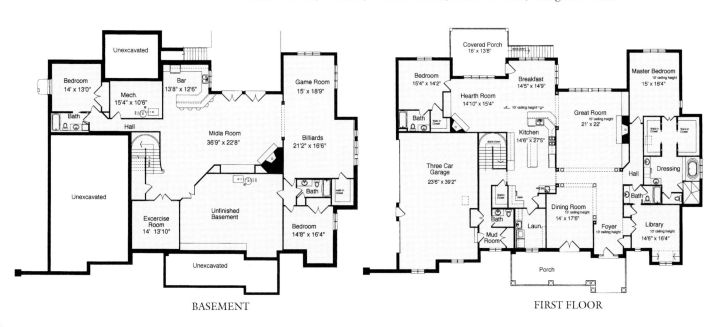

BASEMENT

FIRST FLOOR

DAVID PAPAZIAN

THIS HOME AS SHOWN IN THE PHOTOGRAPH MAY DIFFER FROM THE ACTUAL BLUEPRINTS.

plan# HPT9700026

STYLE: BUNGALOW
FIRST FLOOR: 2,597 SQ. FT.
SECOND FLOOR: 2,171 SQ. FT.
TOTAL: 4,768 SQ. FT.
BEDROOMS: 4
BATHROOMS: 4½
WIDTH: 76' - 6"
DEPTH: 68' - 6"
FOUNDATION: CRAWLSPACE

SEARCH ONLINE @ EPLANS.COM

This splendid Craftsman home will look good in any neighborhood. Inside, the foyer offers a beautiful wooden bench to the right, flanked by built-in curio cabinets. On the left, double French doors lead to a cozy study. The formal dining room is complete with beamed ceilings, a built-in hutch, and cabinets. The large L-shaped kitchen includes a work island/snack bar, plenty of storage, and an adjacent sunny nook. The two-story great room surely lives up to its name, with a massive stone fireplace and a two-story wall of windows. Upstairs, two family bedrooms share a full bath, while the guest suite features its own bath. The lavish master bedroom suite pampers the homeowner with two walk-in closets, a fireplace, and a private deck.

FIRST FLOOR

SECOND FLOOR

plan# HPT9700027

STYLE: CHATEAU
FIRST FLOOR: 3,517 SQ. FT.
SECOND FLOOR: 1,254 SQ. FT.
TOTAL: 4,771 SQ. FT.
BEDROOMS: 5
BATHROOMS: 4½ + ½
WIDTH: 95' - 8"
DEPTH: 107' - 0"
FOUNDATION: SLAB

SEARCH ONLINE @ EPLANS.COM

The design of this French Country estate captures its ambiance with its verandas, grand entry, and unique balconies. A spectacular panorama of the formal living areas and the elegant curved stairway awaits just off the foyer. A large island kitchen, breakfast nook, and family room will impress, as will the wine cellar. Plenty of kitchen pantry space leads to the laundry and motor court featuring a two-car garage attached to the main house and a three-car garage attached by a breezeway. The master suite boasts a sunken sitting area with a see-through fire-place, His and Hers walk-in closets, island tub, and large separate shower. A study area, three additional bedrooms, and a full bath reside on the second floor.

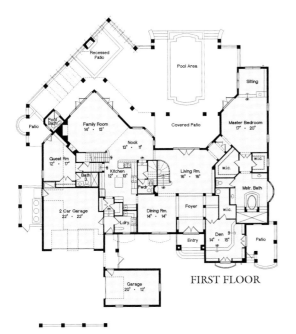

FIRST FLOOR

SECOND FLOOR

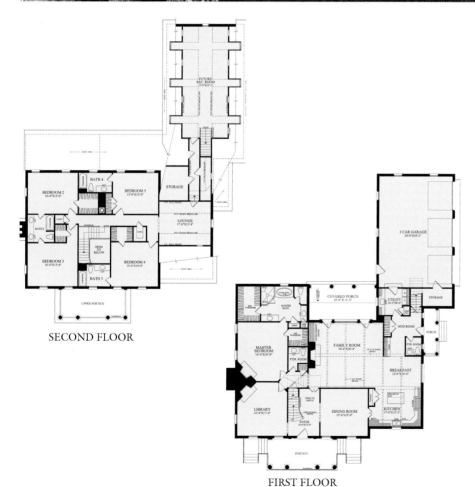

SECOND FLOOR

FIRST FLOOR

plan# HPT9700028

STYLE: SOUTHERN COLONIAL
FIRST FLOOR: 2,670 SQ. FT.
SECOND FLOOR: 1,795 SQ. FT.
TOTAL: 4,465 SQ. FT.
BONUS SPACE: 744 SQ. FT.
BEDROOMS: 5
BATHROOMS: 4½ + ½
WIDTH: 74' - 8"
DEPTH: 93' - 10"
FOUNDATION: CRAWLSPACE,
BASEMENT

SEARCH ONLINE @ EPLANS.COM

A stately brick plantation home, this plan presents all the luxuries that are so desired by today's homeowner. Enter past the columned portico to the formal two-story foyer. To the left is a library with a corner fireplace; to the right, the dining room flows into an enormous kitchen, outfitted with an island serving bar. Exposed wood-beam ceilings in the kitchen, breakfast area, and family room add a vintage element. The master suite is a romantic hideaway, with a corner fireplace, whirlpool tub, and seated shower. Upstairs, four well-appointed bedrooms join a lounge area to finish the plan. Future space above the three-car garage is limited only by your imagination.

plan# HPT9700029

STYLE: PLANTATION
FIRST FLOOR: 2,732 SQ. FT.
SECOND FLOOR: 2,734 SQ. FT.
TOTAL: 5,466 SQ. FT.
BEDROOMS: 5
BATHROOMS: 5½ + ½
WIDTH: 85' - 0"
DEPTH: 85' - 6"
FOUNDATION: CRAWLSPACE,
BASEMENT, SLAB

SEARCH ONLINE @ EPLANS.COM

A wraparound covered porch adds plenty of outdoor space to this already impressive home. Built-in cabinets flank the fireplace in the grand room; a fireplace also warms the hearth room. The gourmet kitchen includes an island counter, large walk-in pantry, and serving bar. A secluded home office, with a separate entrance nearby, provides a quiet work place. A front parlor provides even more room for entertaining or relaxing. The master suite dominates the second floor, offering a spacious sitting area with an elegant tray ceiling, a dressing area, and a luxurious bath with two walk-in closets, double vanities, and a raised garden tub. The second floor is also home to an enormous exercise room and three additional bedrooms.

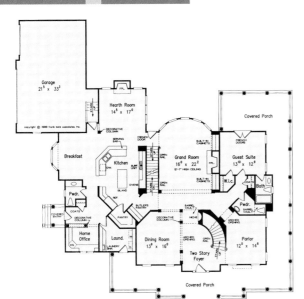

FIRST FLOOR

SECOND FLOOR

plan# HPT9700030

STYLE: FRENCH COUNTRY
FIRST FLOOR: 3,328 SQ. FT.
SECOND FLOOR: 868 SQ. FT.
TOTAL: 4,196 SQ. FT.
BEDROOMS: 5
BATHROOMS: 4
WIDTH: 108' - 2"
DEPTH: 61' - 6"
FOUNDATION: SLAB, CRAWLSPACE

SEARCH ONLINE @ EPLANS.COM

The combination of stucco, stacked stone, and brick adds texture and character to this French Country home. The foyer offers views to the study, dining room, and living room. Double French doors open to the study with built-in bookcases and a window seat overlooking the rear deck. The breakfast room, family room, and spacious kitchen make a nice backdrop for family living. The master suite is enhanced by a raised, corner fireplace, and a bath with an exercise room. Upstairs, two family bedrooms—or make one an office—and a full bath are balanced by a large game room.

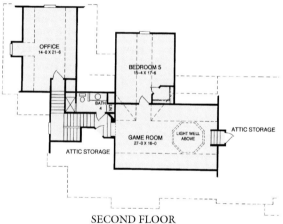

SECOND FLOOR

FIRST FLOOR

plan# HPT9700031

STYLE: CRAFTSMAN
FIRST FLOOR: 2,665 SQ. FT.
SECOND FLOOR: 1,081 SQ. FT.
TOTAL: 3,746 SQ. FT.
BEDROOMS: 4
BATHROOMS: 3½
WIDTH: 88' - 0"
DEPTH: 52' - 6"
FOUNDATION: BASEMENT

SEARCH ONLINE @ EPLANS.COM

This lovely plan steps into the future with an exterior mix of brick, stone, and cedar siding. With a large front porch, the home appears as if it should be located in a quaint oceanfront community. Comfortable elegance coupled with modern-day amenities and nostalgic materials make this home a great choice. The large great room and hearth room/breakfast area offer grand views to the rear yard, where a large deck complements outdoor activities.

FIRST FLOOR

Deck

Dressing

Great Room
20' x 16'

Breakfast/Hearth Room
23'7" x 15'4"

Kitchen
15'8" x 16'6"

Laun.

Three Car Garage
21'2" x 38'5"

Master Bedroom
15' x 19'10"

Library
15'2" x 11'6"

Foyer

Dining Room
13'2" x 13'6"

Porch

SECOND FLOOR

Great Room Below

Computer Loft

Bedroom
13'6" x 16'2"

Bath

Bedroom
13'6" x 14'5"

Foyer Below

Bedroom
13'6" x 13'10"

Bath

PHOTO COURTESY OF LIVING CONCEPTS HOME PLANNING. THIS HOME AS SHOWN IN THE PHOTOGRAPH, MAY DIFFER FROM THE ACTUAL BLUEPRINTS.

plan# HPT9700032

STYLE: FRENCH
FIRST FLOOR: 2,971 SQ. FT.
SECOND FLOOR: 2,199 SQ. FT.
THIRD FLOOR: 1,040 SQ. FT.
TOTAL: 6,210 SQ. FT.
BASEMENT: 1,707 SQ. FT.
BEDROOMS: 5
BATHROOMS: 4½
WIDTH: 84' - 4"
DEPTH: 64' - 11"
FOUNDATION: BASEMENT

SEARCH ONLINE @ EPLANS.COM

SECOND FLOOR

THIRD FLOOR

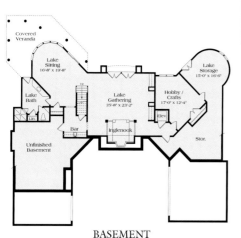

BASEMENT

FIRST FLOOR

Symmetry and stucco present true elegance on the facade of this five-bedroom home, and the elegance continues inside over four separate levels. Note the formal and informal gathering areas on the main level: the music room, the lake living room, the formal dining room, and the uniquely shaped breakfast room. The second level contains three large bedroom suites—one with its own bath—a spacious girl's room for play time and an entrance room to the third-floor master suite. Lavish is the only way to describe this suite. Complete with His and Hers walk-in closets, a private balcony, an off-season closet, and a sumptuous bath, this suite is designed to pamper the homeowner. In the basement is yet more room for casual get-togethers. Note the large sitting room as well as the hobby/crafts room. And tying it all together, an elevator offers stops at each floor.

plan# HPT9700033

STYLE: COLONIAL
FIRST FLOOR: 2,988 SQ. FT.
SECOND FLOOR: 1,216 SQ. FT.
TOTAL: 4,204 SQ. FT.
BONUS SPACE: 485 SQ. FT.
BEDROOMS: 4
BATHROOMS: 4½ + ½
WIDTH: 83' - 0"
DEPTH: 70' - 4"
FOUNDATION: CRAWLSPACE, BASEMENT

SEARCH ONLINE @ EPLANS.COM

Palladian windows, fluted pilasters, and a pedimented entry give this home a distinctly Colonial flavor. Inside, the two-story foyer is flanked by the formal dining and living rooms. The spacious, two-story family room features a fireplace, built-ins, and backyard access. A large country kitchen provides a work island, walk-in pantry, planning desk, and breakfast area. The lavish master suite offers a tremendous amount of closet space, as well as a pampering bath. A nearby study could also serve as a nursery. Upstairs, three bedrooms, each with a private bath, have access to the future recreation room over the garage.

FIRST FLOOR

SECOND FLOOR

Covered porches on both levels welcome all to this fine Plantation-style home. The welcoming atmosphere continues inside, where four fireplaces—in the family room, master bedroom, and living and dining rooms—provide warmth. A screened rear porch, perfect for outdoor dining, is accessible from the family room. The kitchen/breakfast area dazzles with a beamed ceiling, central snack-bar counter, walk-in pantry, and built-in desk. Upstairs, three secondary bedrooms each include a private bath, and the study boasts a dormer alcove. A future recreation room offers space for expansion.

plan# HPT9700034

STYLE: PLANTATION
FIRST FLOOR: 2,696 SQ. FT.
SECOND FLOOR: 1,518 SQ. FT.
TOTAL: 4,214 SQ. FT.
BONUS SPACE: 360 SQ. FT.
BEDROOMS: 4
BATHROOMS: 4½ + ½
WIDTH: 72' - 6"
DEPTH: 97' - 10"
FOUNDATION: CRAWLSPACE

SEARCH ONLINE @ EPLANS.COM

FIRST FLOOR

SECOND FLOOR

plan# HPT9700035

STYLE: FARMHOUSE
FIRST FLOOR: 2,442 SQ. FT.
SECOND FLOOR: 1,286 SQ. FT.
TOTAL: 3,728 SQ. FT.
BONUS SPACE: 681 SQ. FT.
BEDROOMS: 4
BATHROOMS: 3½ + ½
WIDTH: 84' - 8"
DEPTH: 60' - 0"
FOUNDATION: CRAWLSPACE

SEARCH ONLINE @ EPLANS.COM

With a gazebo-style covered porch and careful exterior details, you can't help but imagine tea parties, porch swings, and lazy summer evenings. Inside, a living room/library will comfort with its fireplace and built-ins. The family room is graced with a fireplace and a curved, two-story ceiling with an overlook above. The master bedroom is a private retreat with a lovely bath, twin walk-in closets, and rear-porch access. Upstairs, three bedrooms with sizable closets—one bedroom would make an excellent guest suite or alternate master suite—share access to expandable space.

FIRST FLOOR

SECOND FLOOR

plan# HPT9700036

STYLE: FRENCH
FIRST FLOOR: 2,764 SQ. FT.
SECOND FLOOR: 1,598 SQ. FT.
TOTAL: 4,362 SQ. FT.
BEDROOMS: 4
BATHROOMS: 3½
WIDTH: 74' - 6"
DEPTH: 65' - 10"
FOUNDATION: BASEMENT,
CRAWLSPACE

SEARCH ONLINE @ EPLANS.COM

The heart of this magnificent design is the two-story living room with its fireplace and built-in bookshelves. To the right rear of the plan lie the more casual rooms—the vaulted family room, island kitchen with pantry, and the breakfast nook. A formal dining room awaits elegant meals at the front of the plan. The private master wing features a secluded study, bayed sitting area, and deluxe vaulted bath. Upstairs, three bedrooms, each with ample closet space, share two full baths and a loft and gallery that overlook the first floor.

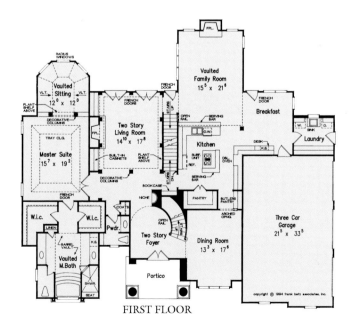

FIRST FLOOR

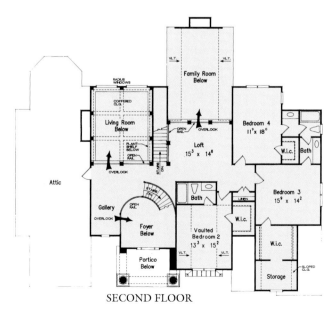

SECOND FLOOR

plan# HPT9700037

STYLE: TRADITIONAL
FIRST FLOOR: 2,617 SQ. FT.
SECOND FLOOR: 1,072 SQ. FT.
TOTAL: 3,689 SQ. FT.
BEDROOMS: 4
BATHROOMS: 4½
WIDTH: 83' - 5"
DEPTH: 73' - 4"

SEARCH ONLINE @ EPLANS.COM

A spectacular volume entry with a curving staircase opens through columns to the formal areas of this home. The sunken living room contains a fireplace, a wet bar, and a bowed window, while the front-facing dining room offers a built-in hutch. The family room, with bookcases surrounding a fireplace, is open to a bayed breakfast nook, and both are easily served from the nearby kitchen. Placed away from the living area of the home, the den provides a quiet retreat. The master suite on the first floor contains an elegant bath and a huge walk-in closet. Second-floor bedrooms also include walk-in closets and private baths.

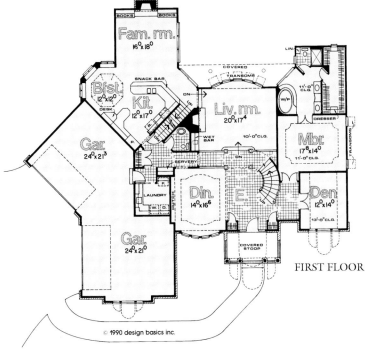

FIRST FLOOR

© 1990 design basics inc.

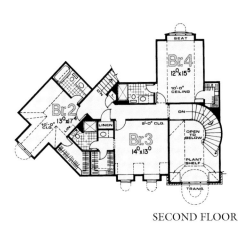

SECOND FLOOR

plan# HPT9700038

Finely crafted porches—front, side, and rear—make this home a classic in traditional Southern living. Past the large French doors, the impressive foyer is flanked by the formal living and dining rooms. Beyond the stair is a vaulted great room with an expanse of windows, a fireplace, and built-in bookcases. From here, the breakfast room and kitchen are easily accessible and open to a private side porch. The master suite provides a large bath, two spacious closets, and a fireplace. The second floor contains three bedrooms with private bath access and a playroom.

STYLE: PLANTATION
FIRST FLOOR: 2,380 SQ. FT.
SECOND FLOOR: 1,295 SQ. FT.
TOTAL: 3,675 SQ. FT.
BEDROOMS: 4
BATHROOMS: 3½
WIDTH: 77' - 4"
DEPTH: 58' - 4"
FOUNDATION: WALKOUT BASEMENT

SEARCH ONLINE @ EPLANS.COM

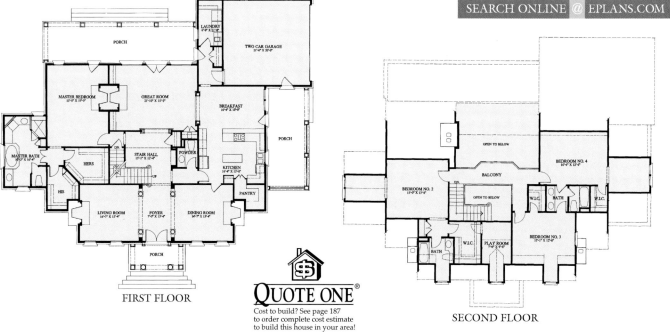

FIRST FLOOR

QUOTE ONE®
Cost to build? See page 187
to order complete cost estimate
to build this house in your area!

SECOND FLOOR

plan# HPT9700039

STYLE: COLONIAL
FIRST FLOOR: 2,273 SQ. FT.
SECOND FLOOR: 1,391 SQ. FT.
TOTAL: 3,664 SQ. FT.
BONUS SPACE: 547 SQ. FT.
BEDROOMS: 4
BATHROOMS: 4½
WIDTH: 77' - 2"
DEPTH: 48' - 0"
FOUNDATION: CRAWLSPACE

SEARCH ONLINE @ EPLANS.COM

Keystone lintels top many of the windows on the facade of this design, adding to its classic Colonial look. A wall of windows brightens the family room, which opens to a spacious rear terrace. Nearby, the kitchen features a central island and easy access to the breakfast area. The master bedroom, which receives natural light from a large bay window, includes a walk-in closet and a private bath with a whirlpool tub, separate shower, and compartmented toilet. Upstairs, three family bedrooms all include private baths, and two boast walk-in closets as well.

FIRST FLOOR

SECOND FLOOR

plan# HPT9700040

STYLE: EUROPEAN COTTAGE
FIRST FLOOR: 3,030 SQ. FT.
SECOND FLOOR: 848 SQ. FT.
TOTAL: 3,878 SQ. FT.
BONUS SPACE: 320 SQ. FT.
BEDROOMS: 4
BATHROOMS: 4½
WIDTH: 88' - 0"
DEPTH: 72' - 1"
FOUNDATION: SLAB

SEARCH ONLINE @ EPLANS.COM

This dazzling and majestic European design features a stucco and stone facade, French shutters, and castle-like rooflines. The entry is flanked by a study with a fireplace and a formal dining room. A formal living room with a fireplace is just across the gallery. The master wing is brightened by a bayed sitting area and features a private bath that extends impressive closet space. The island kitchen overlooks the breakfast and great rooms. A guest suite is located on the first floor for privacy, while two additional family bedrooms reside upstairs, along with a future playroom.

FIRST FLOOR

SECOND FLOOR

plan# HPT9700041

STYLE: EUROPEAN COTTAGE
FIRST FLOOR: 3,033 SQ. FT.
SECOND FLOOR: 1,545 SQ. FT.
TOTAL: 4,578 SQ. FT.
BEDROOMS: 4
BATHROOMS: 3½ + ½
WIDTH: 91' - 6"
DEPTH: 63' - 8"
FOUNDATION: CRAWLSPACE,
SLAB, BASEMENT

SEARCH ONLINE @ EPLANS.COM

This majestic storybook cottage, from the magical setting of rural Europe, provides the perfect home for any large family with a wealth of modern comforts within. A graceful staircase cascades from the two-story foyer. To the left, a sophisticated study offers a wall of built-ins. To the right, a formal dining room is easily served from the island kitchen. The breakfast room accesses the rear screened porch. Fireplaces warm the great room and keeping room. Two sets of double doors open from the great room to the rear covered porch. The master bedroom features private porch access, a sitting area, lavish bath, and two walk-in closets. Upstairs, three additional family bedrooms offer walk-in closet space galore! The game room is great entertainment for both family and friends. A three-car garage with golf-cart storage completes the plan.

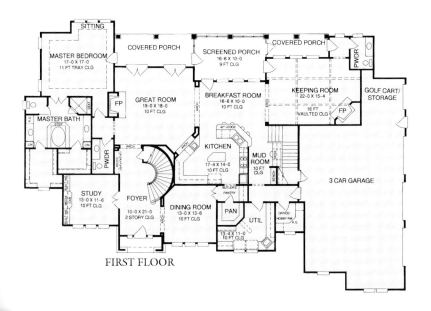

FIRST FLOOR

SECOND FLOOR

This custom-designed estate home elegantly combines stone and stucco, arched windows, and stunning exterior details under its formidable hipped roof. The two-story foyer is impressive with its grand staircase, tray ceiling, and overlooking balcony. Equally remarkable is the generous living room with a fireplace and a coffered two-story ceiling. The kitchen, breakfast bay, and family room with a fireplace are all open to one another for a comfortable, casual atmosphere. The first-floor master suite indulges with numerous closets, a dressing room, and a fabulous bath. Upstairs, four more bedrooms are topped by tray ceilings—three have walk-in closets and two have private baths. The three-car garage boasts additional storage and a bonus room above.

plan# HPT9700042

STYLE: EUROPEAN COTTAGE
FIRST FLOOR: 3,520 SQ. FT.
SECOND FLOOR: 1,638 SQ. FT.
TOTAL: 5,158 SQ. FT.
BONUS SPACE: 411 SQ. FT.
BEDROOMS: 5
BATHROOMS: 4½
WIDTH: 96' - 6"
DEPTH: 58' - 8"

SEARCH ONLINE @ EPLANS.COM

FIRST FLOOR

SECOND FLOOR

© 1998 Donald A. Gardner, Inc.

plan # HPT9700043

STYLE: TRADITIONAL
FIRST FLOOR: 2,908 SQ. FT.
SECOND FLOOR: 1,021 SQ. FT.
TOTAL: 3,929 SQ. FT.
BONUS SPACE: 328 SQ. FT.
BEDROOMS: 5
BATHROOMS: 4
WIDTH: 85' - 4"
DEPTH: 70' - 4"

SEARCH ONLINE @ EPLANS.COM

Siding and stone embellish the exterior of this five-bedroom traditional estate for an exciting, yet stately appearance. A two-story foyer creates an impressive entry. An equally impressive two-story great room features a fireplace, built-ins, and back-porch access. The first-floor master suite enjoys an elegant tray ceiling, back-porch access, and a lavish bath with all the amenities, including an enormous walk-in closet. Down the hall, a second first-floor bedroom converts to a study. The island kitchen easily serves the dining and breakfast rooms. A fireplace warms the casual family room. The breakfast room accesses the screened porch. Three additional bedrooms are on the second floor. The bonus room above the garage is great for attic storage, a home office or a guest suite.

FIRST FLOOR

©1999 Donald A. Gardner, Inc.

SECOND FLOOR

©1998 Donald A. Gardner, Inc.

A variety of exterior materials and interesting windows combine with an unusual floor plan to make this an exceptional home. It is designed for a sloping lot, with full living quarters on the main level, but with two extra bedrooms and a family room added to the lower level. A covered porch showcases a wonderful dining-room window and an attractive front door. The living room, enhanced by a fireplace, adjoins the dining room for easy entertaining. The island kitchen and a bayed breakfast room are to the left. Three bedrooms on this level include one that could serve as a study and one as a master suite with dual vanities, a garden tub, and a walk-in closet. A deck on this floor covers the patio off the lower-level family room, which has its own fireplace.

plan# HPT9700044

STYLE: TRADITIONAL
MAIN LEVEL: 2,297 SQ. FT.
LOWER LEVEL: 1,212 SQ. FT.
TOTAL: 3,509 SQ. FT.
BEDROOMS: 5
BATHROOMS: 5½
WIDTH: 70' - 10"
DEPTH: 69' - 0"

SEARCH ONLINE @ EPLANS.COM

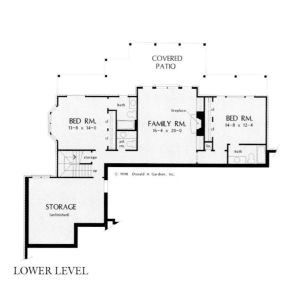

LOWER LEVEL

MAIN LEVEL

© 2000 Donald A. Gardner, Inc.

plan# HPT9700045

STYLE: TRADITIONAL
MAIN LEVEL: 3,040 SQ. FT.
LOWER LEVEL: 1,736 SQ. FT.
TOTAL: 4,776 SQ. FT.
BEDROOMS: 5
BATHROOMS: 4½ + ½
WIDTH: 106' - 1"
DEPTH: 104' - 2"

SEARCH ONLINE @ EPLANS.COM

A modern interpretation of a classic ranch estate, this house plan's exterior features stately columns, decorative wood brackets, and an inviting front porch. Rugged stonework combines with gentle arches in the front clerestory, dormer windows, and entryway to add architectural interest. Inside, decorative ceilings with exposed wood beams top the master bedroom, great room, dining room, and screened porch. This hillside home boasts four fireplaces and a rear wall of windows that capture exceptional views. Other custom-styled elements include a wet bar in the media room and a private study/sitting area in the master suite. Lush yet practical, this home provides an abundance of storage and counter space as seen in the kitchen and laundry/mudroom.

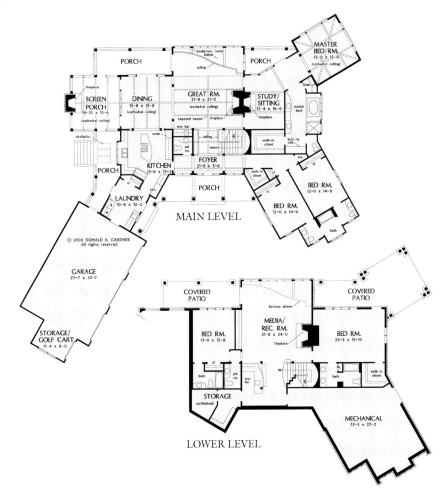

MAIN LEVEL

LOWER LEVEL

plan# HPT9700046

STYLE: BUNGALOW
FIRST FLOOR: 2,391 SQ. FT.
SECOND FLOOR: 1,539 SQ. FT.
TOTAL: 3,930 SQ. FT.
BEDROOMS: 3
BATHROOMS: 3½
WIDTH: 71' - 0"
DEPTH: 69' - 0"
FOUNDATION: BASEMENT

SEARCH ONLINE @ EPLANS.COM

Climate is a key component of any mountain retreat, and outdoor living is an integral part of its design. This superior cabin features open and covered porches. A mix of matchstick details and rugged stone set off this lodge-house facade, concealing a well-defined interior. Windows line the breakfast bay and brighten the kitchen, which features a center cooktop island. A door leads out to a covered porch, a summer kitchen with a built-in grill, and another porch with a cabana bath. The upper level features a secluded master suite with a spacious bath beginning with a double walk-in closet and ending with a garden view of the porch. A two-sided fireplace extends warmth to the whirlpool spa-style tub.

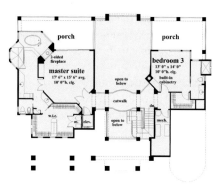

SECOND FLOOR

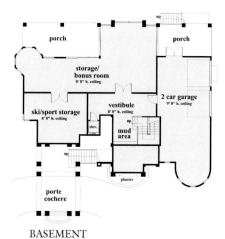

BASEMENT

FIRST FLOOR

plan# HPT9700047 L

STYLE: FLORIDIAN
FIRST FLOOR: 2,725 SQ. FT.
SECOND FLOOR: 1,418 SQ. FT.
TOTAL: 4,143 SQ. FT.
BEDROOMS: 4
BATHROOMS: 5½
WIDTH: 61' - 4"
DEPTH: 62' - 0"
FOUNDATION: BASEMENT

SEARCH ONLINE @ EPLANS.COM

Florida living takes off in this inventive design. A grand room gains attention as a superb entertaining area. A see-through fireplace here connects this room to the dining room. In the study, quiet time is assured—or slip out the doors and onto the veranda for a breather. A full bath connects the study and Bedroom 2. Bedroom 3 sits on the opposite side of the house and enjoys its own bath. The kitchen features a large work island and a connecting breakfast nook. Upstairs, the master bedroom suite contains His and Hers baths, a see-through fireplace, and access to an upper deck. A guest bedroom suite is located on the other side of the upper floor.

Quote One®
Cost to build? See page 187 to order complete cost estimate to build this house in your area!

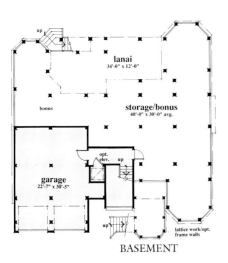

BASEMENT

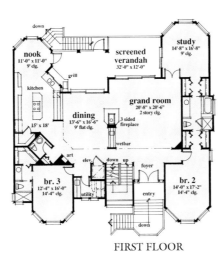

FIRST FLOOR

SECOND FLOOR

© 1989 The Sater Group, Inc.

plan# HPT9700048

STYLE: FLORIDIAN
SQUARE FOOTAGE: 3,896
BONUS SPACE: 356 SQ. FT.
BEDROOMS: 3
BATHROOMS: 4½
WIDTH: 90' - 0"
DEPTH: 120' - 8"
FOUNDATION: SLAB

L

SEARCH ONLINE @ EPLANS.COM

This elegant exterior blends a classical look with a contemporary feel. The formal living room, complete with a fireplace and a wet bar, and the formal dining room access the lanai through three pairs of French doors. The well-appointed kitchen features an island prep sink, a walk-in pantry, and a desk. The secondary bedrooms are full guest suites, located away from the master suite. This suite enjoys enormous His and Hers closets, built-ins, a wet bar, and a three-sided fireplace that separates the sitting room and the bedroom. The luxurious bath features a stunning rounded glass-block shower and a whirlpool tub.

Floor Plan Labels

sitting 12'-0" x 13'-0" 12' tray clg.

master suite 19'-0" x 17'-0" 12' tray clg.

lanai 30'-0" x 14'-0"
outdoor kitchen

leisure 17'-8" x 22'-8" 12' flat clg.

entertainment center

lanai 28'-0" x 9'-0"

nook 12'-0" x 13'-0" 12' flat clg.

hers
his
built ins

built ins
wetbar
glass block shower

living 12'-8" x 16'-8" 13'-4" flat clg.

dining 12'-8" x 16'-8" 13'-4" flat clg.

kitchen 18'-4" x 16'-4"

gallery

grand foyer

gallery

study 13'-0" x 15'-8" 13' tray clg.

entry

guest 15'-4" x 12'-8" 9'-4" flat clg.

guest 13'-0" x 13'-0" 9'-4" flat clg.

planter

planter

utility

garage 23'-0" x 35'-0"

© 1989 The Sater Group, Inc.

bonus 9' x 28'
dormer
dormer

© 1991 The Sater Group, Inc.

plan# HPT9700049

L

STYLE: MEDITERRANEAN
FIRST FLOOR: 4,760 SQ. FT.
SECOND FLOOR: 1,552 SQ. FT.
TOTAL: 6,312 SQ. FT.
BEDROOMS: 5
BATHROOMS: 6½
WIDTH: 98' - 0"
DEPTH: 103' - 8"
FOUNDATION: SLAB

SEARCH ONLINE @ EPLANS.COM

This home features a spectacular blend of arch-top windows, French doors, and balusters. An impressive informal leisure room has a 16-foot tray ceiling, an entertainment center, and a grand wet bar. The large gourmet kitchen is well appointed and easily serves the nook and formal dining room. The master suite has a large bedroom and a bayed sitting area. His and Hers vanities and walk-in closets and a curved glass-block shower are highlights in the bath. The staircase leads to the deluxe secondary guest suites, two of which have observation decks to the rear and each with their own full baths.

QUOTE ONE®

Cost to build? See page 187
to order complete cost estimate
to build this house in your area!

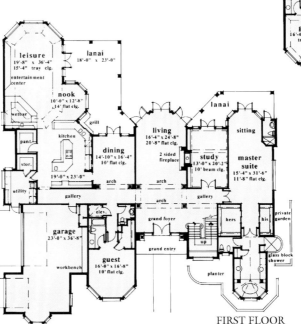

SECOND FLOOR

FIRST FLOOR

THIS HOME AS SHOWN IN THE PHOTOGRAPH, MAY DIFFER FROM THE ACTUAL BLUEPRINTS.

OSCAR THOMPSON

plan# HPT9700050

STYLE: CONTEMPORARY
FIRST FLOOR: 4,470 SQ. FT.
SECOND FLOOR: 680 SQ. FT.
TOTAL: 5,150 SQ. FT.
BEDROOMS: 3
BATHROOMS: 4½
WIDTH: 102' - 0"
DEPTH: 131' - 4"
FOUNDATION: SLAB

SEARCH ONLINE @ EPLANS.COM

The grand entry of this contemporary home gives way to an enticing interior. The living room features a two-story stepped ceiling and access to a covered veranda. The dining room, with a wall of curved glass, allows dramatic views and provides a buffet server for formal events. A leisure room includes a built-in entertainment center, wet bar, and fireplace. Other special features include private gardens for the first-floor guest suite and master suite, a built-in desk in the study, two galleries, an art display niche, and a rear veranda with an outdoor kitchen.

FIRST FLOOR

SECOND FLOOR

plan# HPT9700051

L

STYLE: FLORIDIAN
SQUARE FOOTAGE: 4,187
BEDROOMS: 3
BATHROOMS: 3½
WIDTH: 84' - 8"
DEPTH: 114' - 0"
FOUNDATION: SLAB

SEARCH ONLINE @ EPLANS.COM

This contemporary masterpiece features many luxury details. At the covered entry, a Palladian-style metal grille adds interest. Beyond the foyer, the living room opens up to the lanai through corner sliding glass doors. The informal leisure area is perfect for family gatherings. Full guest suites and an exercise or hobby room are located nearby. The master wing features a study with curved glass, a luxurious bath, and a sitting bay.

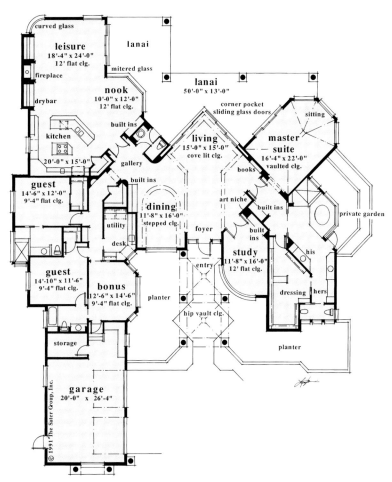

PHOTO COURTESY OF STEPHEN FULLER, INC.
THIS HOME AS SHOWN IN THE PHOTOGRAPH, MAY DIFFER FROM THE ACTUAL BLUEPRINTS.

A symmetrical facade with twin chimneys makes a grand statement. A covered porch welcomes visitors and provides a pleasant place to spend a mild evening. The entry is flanked by formal living areas—a dining room and a living room—each with a fireplace. A third fireplace is the highlight of the expansive great room to the rear. An L-shaped kitchen offers a work island and a walk-in pantry and easily serves the nearby breakfast area and sunroom. The master suite provides lavish luxuries.

plan# HPT9700052

STYLE: TRADITIONAL
FIRST FLOOR: 2,565 SQ. FT.
SECOND FLOOR: 1,375 SQ. FT.
TOTAL: 3,940 SQ. FT.
BEDROOMS: 4
BATHROOMS: 3½
WIDTH: 88' - 6"
DEPTH: 58' - 6"
FOUNDATION: WALKOUT
BASEMENT

SEARCH ONLINE @ EPLANS.COM

FIRST FLOOR

SECOND FLOOR

...MAY DIFFER FROM THE ACTUAL BLUEPRINTS. FOR MORE DETAILED INFORMATION, PLEASE CHECK THE FLOOR PLANS CAREFULLY.

plan# HPT9700053

STYLE: TERRITORIAL
FIRST FLOOR: 3,166 SQ. FT.
SECOND FLOOR: 950 SQ. FT.
TOTAL: 4,116 SQ. FT.
BEDROOMS: 5
BATHROOMS: 4
WIDTH: 154' - 0"
DEPTH: 94' - 8"
FOUNDATION: SLAB

L

SEARCH ONLINE @ EPLANS.COM

A long low-pitched roof distinguishes this Southwestern-style farmhouse design. The tiled entrance leads to a grand dining room and opens to a formal parlor secluded by half-walls. A country kitchen with a cooktop island overlooks the two-story gathering room with its full wall of glass, fireplace, and built-in media shelves. The master suite satisfies the most discerning tastes with a raised hearth, an adjacent study or exercise room, access to the wraparound porch, and a bath with corner whirlpool tub. Rooms upstairs can serve as secondary bedrooms for family members, be converted to home office space, or used as guest bedrooms.

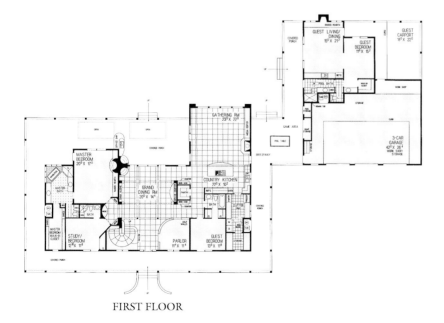

FIRST FLOOR

QUOTE ONE®
Cost to build? See page 187 to order complete cost estimate to build this house in your area!

SECOND FLOOR

Multipane windows and a natural stone facade complement this French Country estate. A two-story foyer leads to a central grand room. A formal dining room to the front offers a fireplace. To the left, a cozy study with a second fireplace features built-in cabinetry. The sleeping quarters offer luxurious amenities. The master bath includes a whirlpool tub in a bumped-out bay, twin lavatories, and two walk-in closets. Upstairs, three suites, each with a walk-in closet and one with its own bath, share a balcony hall. A home theater beckons family and friends toward the back of the second floor. An apartment over the garage will house visiting or live-in relatives or may be used as a maid's quarters.

plan# HPT9700054

STYLE: FRENCH COUNTRY
FIRST FLOOR: 3,560 SQ. FT.
SECOND FLOOR: 1,783 SQ. FT.
TOTAL: 5,343 SQ. FT.
BONUS SPACE: 641 SQ. FT.
BEDROOMS: 4
BATHROOMS: 3½
WIDTH: 121' - 2"
DEPTH: 104' - 4"
FOUNDATION: CRAWLSPACE

SEARCH ONLINE @ EPLANS.COM

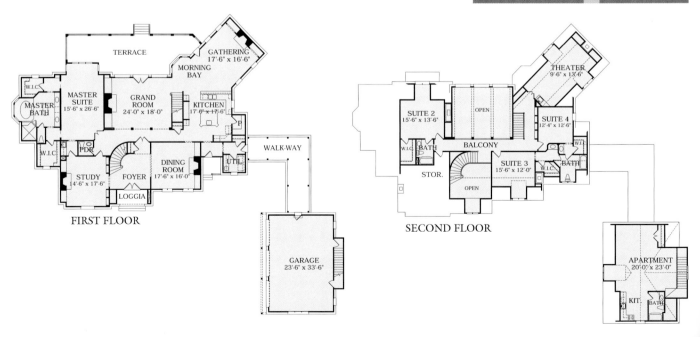

FIRST FLOOR

SECOND FLOOR

plan# HPT9700055

STYLE: COUNTRY COTTAGE
FIRST FLOOR: 3,347 SQ. FT.
SECOND FLOOR: 1,696 SQ. FT.
TOTAL: 5,043 SQ. FT.
BONUS SPACE: 715 SQ. FT.
BEDROOMS: 5
BATHROOMS: 6½
WIDTH: 120' - 0"
DEPTH: 99' - 11"
FOUNDATION: CRAWLSPACE

SEARCH ONLINE @ EPLANS.COM

Gently flaring eaves and curved dormers contrast with the straight rooflines and angled gables on this attractive stone exterior. A breezeway connects the house to the three-car garage, above which an apartment offers living space for a mother-in-law or grown child. On the second floor of the main house, you'll find three more bedroom suites, a sewing room, and a future exercise room. Downstairs, the foyer opens to the formal dining room and leads ahead to the grand room, elegant and inviting with its massive fireplace, built-ins, and French doors to the terrace. A large informal area features a second fireplace and includes a gathering room, a break-fast nook, and an island kitchen with a huge walk-in pantry. Amenities in the master suite include two walk-in closets, a corner garden tub, and dual vanities. A wet bar is shared with the nearby study, which boasts a third fireplace.

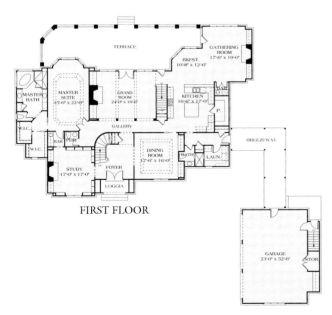

FIRST FLOOR

SECOND FLOOR

© The Sater Design Collection, Inc.

An impressive Italian Renaissance manor, this stone-and-stucco home is stunning from the curb and pure rapture inside. Twin bays at the front of the plan hold a study with a star-stepped ceiling and a dining room with coffer accents and decorative columns. The great room offers a warming fireplace and a soaring coffered ceiling. Not to be missed: an outdoor kitchen in addition to the modern country kitchen and bayed breakfast nook inside. The master suite is a dream come true; a large bay window, oversize walk-in closets, and a pampering bath with a corner tub will delight. Upstairs, three bedrooms all have private baths and large walk-in closets. Two bedrooms enjoy deck access.

plan # HPT9700056

STYLE: FRENCH
FIRST FLOOR: 2,232 SQ. FT.
SECOND FLOOR: 1,269 SQ. FT.
TOTAL: 3,501 SQ. FT.
BEDROOMS: 4
BATHROOMS: 4½
WIDTH: 63' - 9"
DEPTH: 80' - 0"
FOUNDATION: SLAB

SEARCH ONLINE @ EPLANS.COM

FIRST FLOOR

SECOND FLOOR

plan# HPT9700057

STYLE: MEDITERRANEAN
FIRST FLOOR: 3,592 SQ. FT.
SECOND FLOOR: 2,861 SQ. FT.
TOTAL: 6,453 SQ. FT.
BEDROOMS: 5
BATHROOMS: 5½
WIDTH: 96' - 5"
DEPTH: 91' - 6"
FOUNDATION: CRAWLSPACE

SEARCH ONLINE @ EPLANS.COM

Stunning Mediterranean style gives this home a sense of palatial elegance. Arches frame the portico, which leads inside to an impressive two-story foyer—a study warmed by a fireplace is to the left, while a formal dining room is introduced to the right. The first-floor master suite enjoys a deluxe whirlpool bath and two walk-in closets. The island kitchen opens to the casual family room, warmed by a second fireplace. Four additional suites reside upstairs for other family members. A romantic overlook views the great room and foyer. A sitting room is placed just outside of the second-floor recreation room.

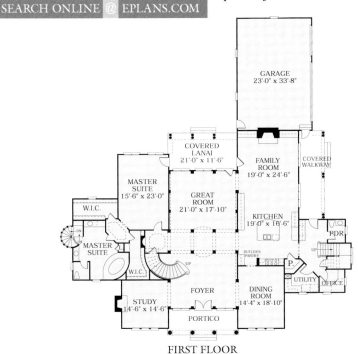

FIRST FLOOR

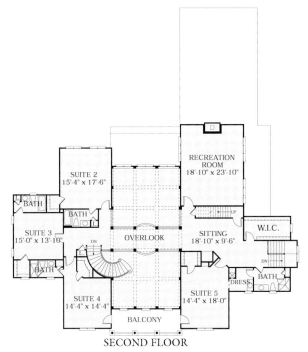

SECOND FLOOR

GOURMET KITCHENS

© The Sater Design Collection, Inc.

Stone, stucco, and soaring rooflines combine to give this elegant Mediterranean design a stunning exterior. The interior is packed with luxurious amenities, from the wall of glass in the living room to the whirlpool tub in the master bath. The spacious island kitchen includes a stepped ceiling, walk-in pantry, and nearby bayed breakfast nook. A dining room and study serve as formal areas, while a leisure room with a fireplace offers a relaxing retreat. The first-floor master suite boasts a private bayed sitting area. Upstairs, all three bedrooms include private baths; Bedroom 2 and the guest suite also provide walk-in closets.

plan# HPT9700058

STYLE: EUROPEAN COTTAGE
FIRST FLOOR: 2,850 SQ. FT.
SECOND FLOOR: 1,155 SQ. FT.
TOTAL: 4,005 SQ. FT.
BONUS SPACE: 371 SQ. FT.
BEDROOMS: 4
BATHROOMS: 4½
WIDTH: 71' - 6"
DEPTH: 83' - 0"
FOUNDATION: SLAB

SEARCH ONLINE @ EPLANS.COM

FIRST FLOOR

SECOND FLOOR

plan# HPT9700059

STYLE: TRADITIONAL
FIRST FLOOR: 2,285 SQ. FT.
SECOND FLOOR: 1,395 SQ. FT.
TOTAL: 3,680 SQ. FT.
BONUS SPACE: 300 SQ. FT.
BEDROOMS: 3
BATHROOMS: 3½
WIDTH: 73' - 8"
DEPTH: 76' - 2"
FOUNDATION: SLAB

SEARCH ONLINE @ EPLANS.COM

Now here is a one-of-a-kind house plan. Step down from the raised foyer into the grand gallery where columns define the living room. This central living area boasts an enormous bow window with a fantastic view to the covered patio. The formal dining room is to the right and the lavish master suite sits on the left. The family gourmet will find an expansive kitchen, with plenty of counter space and a walk-in pantry, beyond a pair of French doors on the right. The secluded family room completes this first level. An enormous den is found on the first landing above, to the left of the foyer. Two bedroom suites and a loft occupy the second floor.

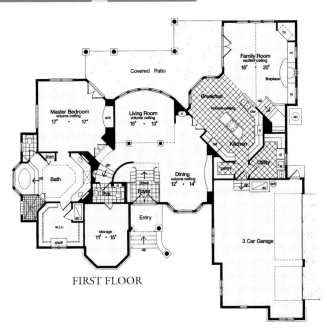

FIRST FLOOR

SECOND FLOOR

plan# HPT9700060

STYLE: MEDITERRANEAN
FIRST FLOOR: 3,027 SQ. FT.
SECOND FLOOR: 1,079 SQ. FT.
TOTAL: 4,106 SQ. FT.
BEDROOMS: 4
BATHROOMS: 3½
WIDTH: 87' - 4"
DEPTH: 80' - 4"
FOUNDATION: BASEMENT

SEARCH ONLINE @ EPLANS.COM

The inside of this design is just as majestic as the outside. The grand foyer opens to a two-story living room with a fireplace and magnificent views. Dining in the bayed formal dining room will be a memorable experience. A well-designed kitchen is near a sunny nook and a leisure room with a fireplace and outdoor access. The master wing includes a separate study and an elegant private bath. The second level features a guest suite with its own bath and deck, two family bedrooms (Bedroom 3 also has its own deck), and a gallery loft with views to the living room below.

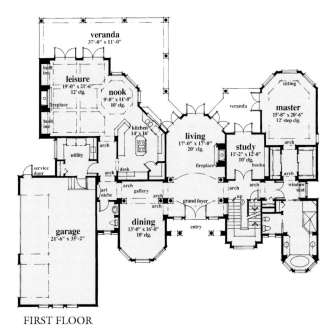

FIRST FLOOR

SECOND FLOOR

ORDER BLUEPRINTS 24 HOURS, 7 DAYS A WEEK, AT 1-800-521-6797

plan# HPT9700061

STYLE: FRENCH
FIRST FLOOR: 2,384 SQ. FT.
SECOND FLOOR: 1,234 SQ. FT.
TOTAL: 3,618 SQ. FT.
BONUS SPACE: 344 SQ. FT.
BEDROOMS: 5
BATHROOMS: 4½
WIDTH: 64' - 6"
DEPTH: 57' - 10"
FOUNDATION: CRAWLSPACE,
BASEMENT, SLAB

SEARCH ONLINE @ EPLANS.COM

Stucco and stone, French shutters, a turret-style bay, and lovely arches create a magical timeless style. A formal arch romanticizes the front entry, which opens to a two-story foyer. A bayed living room resides to the right, and a formal dining room is set to the left. Straight ahead, the vaulted two-story family room is warmed by an enchanting fireplace. The island kitchen is set between the breakfast and dining rooms. The master suite is enhanced by a tray ceiling and offers a lavish master bath with a whirlpool tub. Upstairs, Bedroom 2 offers another private bath and a walk-in closet. Bedrooms 3 and 4 each provide their own walk-in closets and share a full bath between them. The bonus room is perfect for a future home office or playroom.

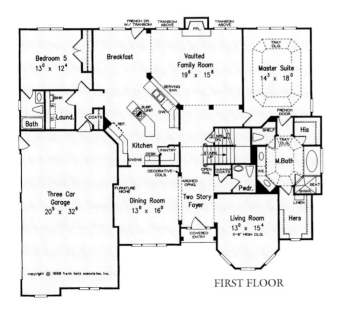

FIRST FLOOR

SECOND FLOOR

A two-story foyer with an elegant curved staircase gives this classic Georgian design an impressive entry. To the left of the foyer, the library boasts a fireplace and built-in shelves. Another fireplace is found in the two-story family room, which accesses the rear terrace. The gourmet kitchen, with a central snack-bar island, opens to a large dining terrace that's perfect for outdoor entertaining. A bay window brightens the opulent master suite. A utility room, discreetly tucked away near the kitchen, features plenty of counter space and a storage area. Upstairs, find three bedrooms, two full baths, and a spacious bonus area reserved for a future recreation room.

plan# HPT9700062

STYLE: GEORGIAN
FIRST FLOOR: 2,767 SQ. FT.
SECOND FLOOR: 1,179 SQ. FT.
TOTAL: 3,946 SQ. FT.
BONUS SPACE: 591 SQ. FT.
BEDROOMS: 4
BATHROOMS: 3½
WIDTH: 79' - 11"
DEPTH: 80' - 6"
FOUNDATION: CRAWLSPACE

SEARCH ONLINE @ EPLANS.COM

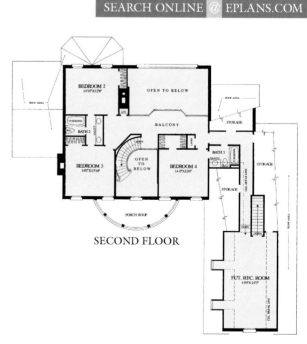

FIRST FLOOR

SECOND FLOOR

plan# HPT9700063

STYLE: COLONIAL
FIRST FLOOR: 2,327 SQ. FT.
SECOND FLOOR: 1,431 SQ. FT.
TOTAL: 3,758 SQ. FT.
BONUS SPACE: 473 SQ. FT.
BEDROOMS: 5
BATHROOMS: 3½
WIDTH: 78' - 10"
DEPTH: 58' - 2"
FOUNDATION: CRAWLSPACE, BASEMENT

SEARCH ONLINE @ EPLANS.COM

This Early American classic was built with attention to the needs of an active family. The formal entrance allows guests to come and go in splendor, and family members can kick off their shoes in the mudroom. The step-saving kitchen is accented by an island for dinner preparations or school projects, and a pantry with tons of space. In the master suite, homeowners can relax in the whirlpool tub and revel in the ample walk-in closet. Second-floor family bedrooms provide privacy, walk-in closets, and two shared baths, both with dual vanities.

plan# **HPT9700064**

A curved front porch, graceful symmetry in the details, and the sturdiness of brick all combine to enhance this beautiful two-story home. Inside, the two-story foyer introduces the formal rooms—the living room to the right and the dining room to the left—and presents the elegant stairwell. The L-shaped kitchen provides a walk-in pantry, an island with a sink, a butler's pantry, and an adjacent breakfast area. Perfect for casual gatherings, the family room features a fireplace and backyard access. Located on the first floor for privacy, the master suite offers a large walk-in closet and a lavish bath. Upstairs, four bedrooms—each with a walk-in closet—share two full baths and access to the future recreation room over the garage.

STYLE: SOUTHERN COLONIAL
FIRST FLOOR: 2,416 SQ. FT.
SECOND FLOOR: 1,535 SQ. FT.
TOTAL: 3,951 SQ. FT.
BONUS SPACE: 552 SQ. FT.
BEDROOMS: 5
BATHROOMS: 3½
WIDTH: 79' - 2"
DEPTH: 63' - 6"
FOUNDATION: CRAWLSPACE,
BASEMENT

SEARCH ONLINE @ EPLANS.COM

FIRST FLOOR

SECOND FLOOR

© 2001 Donald A. Gardner, Inc.

plan# HPT9700065

STYLE: TRADITIONAL
FIRST FLOOR: 2,511 SQ. FT.
SECOND FLOOR: 1,062 SQ. FT.
TOTAL: 3,573 SQ. FT.
BONUS SPACE: 465 SQ. FT.
BEDROOMS: 4
BATHROOMS: 3½
WIDTH: 84' - 11"
DEPTH: 55' - 11"

SEARCH ONLINE @ EPLANS.COM

An abundance of windows and an attractive brick facade enhance the exterior of this traditional two-story home. Inside, a study and formal dining room flank either side of the two-story foyer. Fireplaces warm both the great room and first-floor master suite. The suite also provides a separate sitting room, two walk-in closets, and a private bath. The island kitchen extends into the breakfast room. The second floor features three additional family bedrooms, two baths, and a bonus room fit for a home office.

SECOND FLOOR

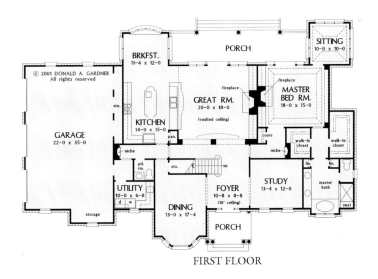

FIRST FLOOR

plan# HPT9700066

STYLE: TRANSITIONAL
FIRST FLOOR: 2,588 SQ. FT.
SECOND FLOOR: 1,375 SQ. FT.
TOTAL: 3,963 SQ. FT.
BONUS SPACE: 460 SQ. FT.
BEDROOMS: 4
BATHROOMS: 3½
WIDTH: 91' - 4"
DEPTH: 51' - 10"
FOUNDATION: CRAWLSPACE

SEARCH ONLINE @ EPLANS.COM

Though there are two entrances to this fine home, the one on the right is where friends and family should enter to truly absorb the grandeur of this design. The foyer is flanked by a bayed formal dining room and a bayed formal living room. Directly ahead is the lake gathering room, a spacious area with a welcoming fireplace and access to the rear veranda. The L-shaped kitchen, complete with an island, includes plenty of space and convenient features like a wet bar, walk-in pantry, and built-in shelves. Located on the first floor for privacy, the master suite is complete with a huge dressing closet, access to the veranda, and a lavish bath.

SECOND FLOOR

FIRST FLOOR

plan# HPT9700067

STYLE: FARMHOUSE
FIRST FLOOR: 1,999 SQ. FT.
SECOND FLOOR: 2,046 SQ. FT.
TOTAL: 4,045 SQ. FT.
BEDROOMS: 5
BATHROOMS: 4½
WIDTH: 66' - 4"
DEPTH: 64' - 0"
FOUNDATION: CRAWLSPACE,
BASEMENT

SEARCH ONLINE @ EPLANS.COM

This luxury farmhouse design is reserved for the hardworking homeowner who seeks a relaxing retreat. A front covered porch that wraps around the side adds a country accent to the exterior. Inside, a study and formal dining room flank the two-story foyer. A guest suite is placed to the right of the two-story family room, warmed by a fireplace. The kitchen, with a wine rack, spacious walk-in pantry, and serving bar, is open to the nook and casual keeping room. A three-car garage is located nearby. Upstairs, the master suite features a hearth-warmed sitting room, private bath, and two large walk-in closets.

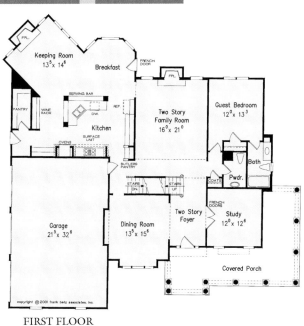

FIRST FLOOR

SECOND FLOOR

© The Sater Design Collection, Inc.

plan# HPT9700068

STYLE: EUROPEAN COTTAGE
SQUARE FOOTAGE: 3,640
BEDROOMS: 3
BATHROOMS: 3½
WIDTH: 106' - 4"
DEPTH: 102' - 4"
FOUNDATION: SLAB

SEARCH ONLINE @ EPLANS.COM

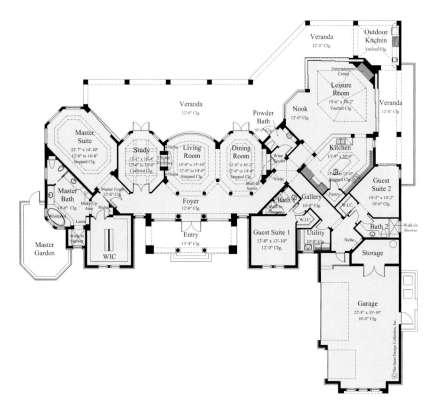

No matter how long your wish list is, you're in luck—this French Colonial home has it all! An unassuming facade is accented by a columned portico entry and a box-bay window. An elongated foyer leads to the elegant living areas: the octagonal study and dining room. Each has a distinctive ceiling treatment; both lead to the rear veranda through French doors. Between them, the living room, with a bowed window wall, shares a two-way fireplace with the study. Don't miss the built-in serving area and wine cooler in the dining room, and the stepped ceiling and walk-in pantry in the kitchen. The unique leisure room includes a bayed nook, perfect for a reading area, and a built-in entertainment center. An outdoor kitchen is a remarkable addition. The left wing is devoted to the comfort of the master suite, where a luxurious bath with a corner whirlpool tub, an unbelievable walk-in closet, and a private garden provide sanctuary.

plan# HPT9700069

STYLE: COUNTRY COTTAGE
FIRST FLOOR: 2,495 SQ. FT.
SECOND FLOOR: 1,233 SQ. FT.
TOTAL: 3,728 SQ. FT.
BONUS SPACE: 351 SQ. FT.
BEDROOMS: 4
BATHROOMS: 3½
WIDTH: 66' - 10"
DEPTH: 57' - 6"
FOUNDATION: BASEMENT,
CRAWLSPACE

SEARCH ONLINE @ EPLANS.COM

The brick-and-siding exterior and hipped roof lend a country aura to this home. Amenities abound inside, including a walk-in pantry and serving bar in the island kitchen and fireplaces in the family and keeping rooms. Vaulted ceilings enhance the family and living rooms, and the keeping room features a lovely bay window. Note the elegant master suite on the first floor and three family bedrooms on the second. An optional bonus room offers plenty of space for future expansion.

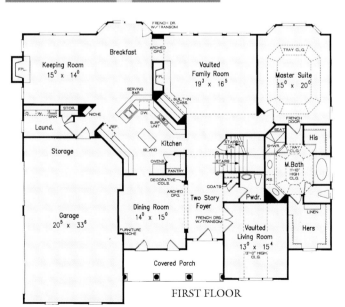

FIRST FLOOR

SECOND FLOOR

plan# HPT9700070

STYLE: PLANTATION
FIRST FLOOR: 3,635 SQ. FT.
SECOND FLOOR: 1,357 SQ. FT.
TOTAL: 4,992 SQ. FT.
BEDROOMS: 4
BATHROOMS: 4½ + ½
WIDTH: 121' - 6"
DEPTH: 60' - 4"
FOUNDATION: CRAWLSPACE,
BASEMENT

SEARCH ONLINE @ EPLANS.COM

The grandeur of this Southern estate belies the practical floor plan within. An elegant foyer joins the dining room and oversized living room—both with fireplaces—to welcome guests. The left wing comprises a gourmet kitchen with a walk-in pantry, two powder rooms, and a utility area featuring a mudroom and a separate entrance. The two-story family room, with porch access and a fireplace, is central; the right wing is devoted to a luxurious master suite and a private study, each with a fireplace. An expansive upper level includes three family suites, a balcony overlook, and future space for a fifth bedroom and bath, as well as a game room.

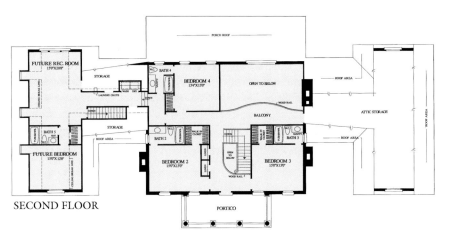

SECOND FLOOR

FIRST FLOOR

plan# HPT9700071

STYLE: FEDERAL
FIRST FLOOR: 3,505 SQ. FT.
SECOND FLOOR: 1,302 SQ. FT.
TOTAL: 4,807 SQ. FT.
BEDROOMS: 5
BATHROOMS: 4½
WIDTH: 89' - 4"
DEPTH: 87' - 0"
FOUNDATION: SLAB

SEARCH ONLINE @ EPLANS.COM

This majestic Early American mansion presents a sturdy, formal outside appearance; inside, it is especially well suited for a large family that likes big informal get-togethers. The huge family room, with a corner fireplace that merges with a dining nook and adjoins the country-style kitchen, will surely be the center of activity. Note the large central island and walk-in pantry in the kitchen. Five bedrooms are placed throughout the home's two levels, including a glorious master suite with all the comforts you've ever dreamed about. A game room joins three bedrooms upstairs. For formal socializing, the dining area and living room are easily entered from the foyer, which guests reach through the impressive pillars of the covered entry. A den, or make it a study, is also located near the front. To the rear is a covered patio, perfect for meals alfresco.

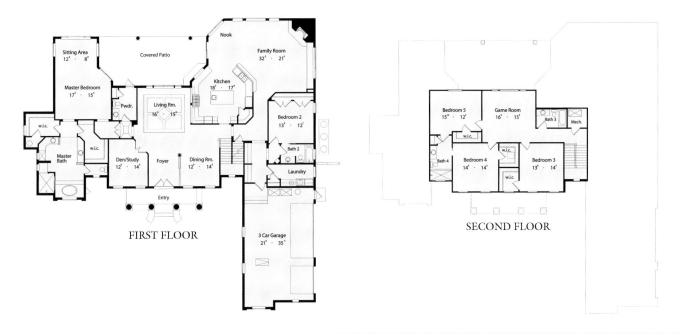

FIRST FLOOR

SECOND FLOOR

plan# **HPT9700072**

STYLE: ITALIANATE
SQUARE FOOTAGE: 3,589
BONUS SPACE: 430 SQ. FT.
BEDROOMS: 4
BATHROOMS: 4
WIDTH: 76' - 0"
DEPTH: 98' - 0"
FOUNDATION: SLAB

SEARCH ONLINE @ EPLANS.COM

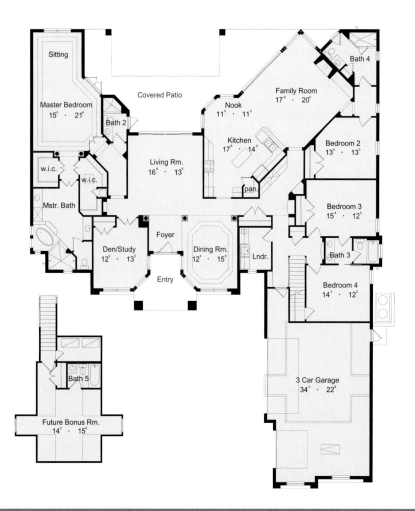

Exquisite rooflines and arched front windows offer a hint of the marvelous treasures to be found inside this European-style beauty. A highlight is the spacious country-style kitchen with lots and lots of counter space—including a handy island—a walk-in pantry, a sunlit breakfast bay, and a wide opening to the family room. The charming master suite encompasses the entire left side of the home. Off the bedchamber is a sitting room with access to a covered rear patio and two ample walk-in closets. The master bath pampers with a shower big enough for two, an oversize tub, two vanities, and a compartmented toilet. On the opposite side of the house, three bedrooms and two baths provide sleeping quarters for family or visitors. A window wall offers views from the living room to the rear patio and gardens.

© 91 HOME DESIGN SERVICES, INC.

plan# HPT9700073

STYLE: FLORIDIAN
SQUARE FOOTAGE: 3,743
BEDROOMS: 4
BATHROOMS: 3½
WIDTH: 86' - 8"
DEPTH: 95' - 0"
FOUNDATION: SLAB

SEARCH ONLINE @ EPLANS.COM

A central foyer gives way to an expansive design. Straight ahead, the living room features French doors set in a bay area. To the left, columns and a coffered ceiling offset the exquisite formal dining room. A fireplace warms the large family room, which adjoins the breakfast nook. Traffic flows easily through the ample kitchen with a cooktop island and pass-through to the patio. The master bedroom features a tray ceiling, walk-in closet, and sumptuous bath with shower and step-up tub overlooking a private garden. Two bedrooms are joined by an optional media room and optional study, which could bring the count up to five bedrooms if necessary.

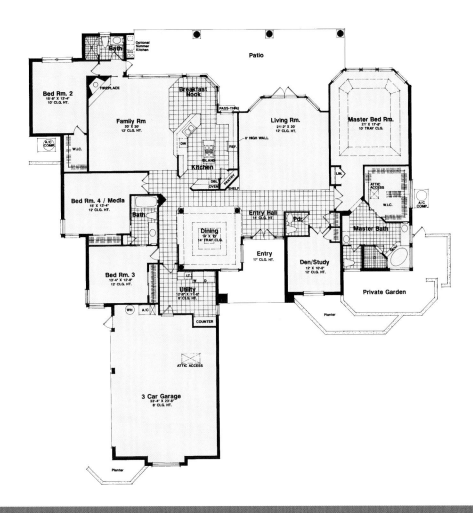

With 10-foot wood-beam ceilings on the first floor and nine-foot ceilings upstairs, this Dutch Colonial offers plenty of aesthetic appeal. Enter the foyer to a dining room with an arched entrance on the left, and to the right, a living room/library with transom pocket doors and a fireplace. The kitchen is full of modern amenities, including an island with a vegetable sink and a snack bar. The master wing provides peace and quiet—and a few surprises! Details like a window seat, whirlpool tub, and storage space make it a welcome retreat. Upstairs, three bedroom suites, each with a private bath, offer room for family and guests. Future space is available for expansion.

plan# HPT9700074

STYLE: COLONIAL
FIRST FLOOR: 3,016 SQ. FT.
SECOND FLOOR: 1,283 SQ. FT.
TOTAL: 4,299 SQ. FT.
BONUS SPACE: 757 SQ. FT.
BEDROOMS: 4
BATHROOMS: 4½ + ½
WIDTH: 105' - 0"
DEPTH: 69' - 0"
FOUNDATION: CRAWLSPACE

SEARCH ONLINE @ EPLANS.COM

FIRST FLOOR

SECOND FLOOR

plan # HPT9700075

STYLE: SOUTHERN COLONIAL
FIRST FLOOR: 3,170 SQ. FT.
SECOND FLOOR: 1,914 SQ. FT.
TOTAL: 5,084 SQ. FT.
BONUS SPACE: 445 SQ. FT.
BEDROOMS: 4
BATHROOMS: 3½
WIDTH: 100' - 10"
DEPTH: 65' - 5"
FOUNDATION: CRAWLSPACE

SEARCH ONLINE @ EPLANS.COM

This elegantly appointed home is a beauty inside and out. A centerpiece stair rises gracefully from the two-story grand foyer. The kitchen, breakfast room, and family room provide open space for the gathering of family and friends. The beam-ceilinged study and the dining room flank the grand foyer and each includes a fireplace. The master bedroom features a cozy sitting area and a luxury master bath with His and Hers vanities and walk-in closets. Three large bedrooms and a game room complete the second floor. A large expandable area is available at the top of the rear stair.

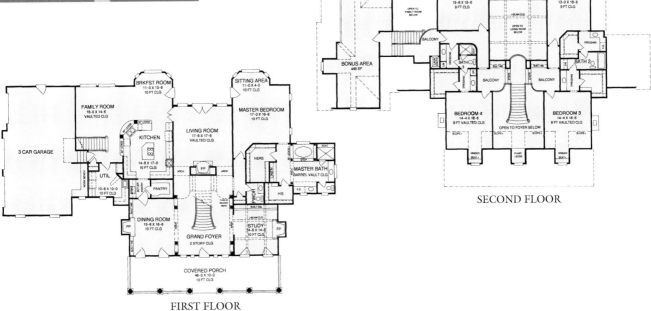

FIRST FLOOR

SECOND FLOOR

plan# HPT9700076

STYLE: COLONIAL
FIRST FLOOR: 2,993 SQ. FT.
SECOND FLOOR: 1,452 SQ. FT.
TOTAL: 4,445 SQ. FT.
BONUS SPACE: 611 SQ. FT.
BEDROOMS: 4
BATHROOMS: 5
WIDTH: 113' - 0"
DEPTH: 65' - 4"
FOUNDATION: CRAWLSPACE

SEARCH ONLINE @ EPLANS.COM

Four dormer windows, a columned front porch, and a gambrel-roofed garage add Colonial style to this sprawling plan. The central family room, which opens to the terrace, provides a great gathering spot. Nearby, the stunning kitchen features a built-in desk and a central island with a sink. The breakfast area and sunroom sit to either side. The master bedroom provides luxury with two walk-in closets and a bath with a whirlpool tub; upstairs, three family bedrooms also boast private baths and walk-in closets.

FIRST FLOOR

SECOND FLOOR

MAGNIFICENT MASTER SUITES

©1998 Donald A. Gardner, Inc.

Brimming with luxury and style, this gracious country estate features spacious rooms, volume ceilings, and four porches for extended outdoor living. Fireplaces in the living and family rooms grant warmth and character to these spacious gathering areas; columns add definition to the open living and dining rooms. Built-in bookshelves in the living room are both attractive and functional, as is the built-in desk adjacent to the open U-shaped staircase. The master suite is a haven with a tray ceiling, a sitting alcove, dual walk-in closets, and a luxurious bath. The upstairs balcony overlooks both the foyer and living room and serves as an open, central hallway for the home's three family bedrooms and bonus room.

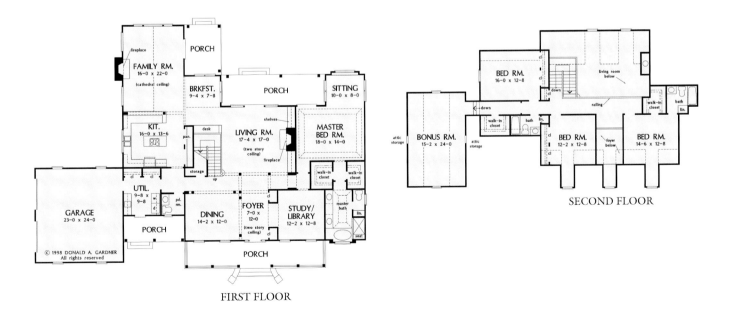

FIRST FLOOR

SECOND FLOOR

plan # HPT9700078

STYLE: COLONIAL
FIRST FLOOR: 2,492 SQ. FT.
SECOND FLOOR: 1,313 SQ. FT.
TOTAL: 3,805 SQ. FT.
BONUS SPACE: 687 SQ. FT.
BEDROOMS: 4
BATHROOMS: 3½ + ½
WIDTH: 85' - 10"
DEPTH: 54' - 6"
FOUNDATION: CRAWLSPACE, BASEMENT

SEARCH ONLINE @ EPLANS.COM

Although the exterior of this Georgian home is entirely classical, the interior boasts an up-to-date floor plan that's a perfect fit for today's lifestyles. The large central family room, conveniently near the kitchen and breakfast area, includes a fireplace and access to the rear terrace; fireplaces also grace the formal dining room and library. The master suite, also with terrace access, features a spacious walk-in closet and a bath with a whirlpool tub. Upstairs, a second master suite—great for guests— joins two family bedrooms. Nearby, a large open area can serve as a recreation room.

FIRST FLOOR

SECOND FLOOR

plan ⊕ HPT9700079

STYLE: COLONIAL 〔L〕〔D〕
FIRST FLOOR: 2,126 SQ. FT.
SECOND FLOOR: 1,882 SQ. FT.
TOTAL: 4,008 SQ. FT.
BEDROOMS: 4
BATHROOMS: 2½
WIDTH: 92' - 0"
DEPTH: 64' - 4"
FOUNDATION: BASEMENT

SEARCH ONLINE @ EPLANS.COM

This historical Georgian home has its roots in the 18th Century. The full two-story center section is delightfully complemented by the 1½-story wings. An elegant gathering room, three steps down from the rest of the house, provides ample space for entertaining on a grand scale. The study and the formal dining room flank the foyer. Each of these rooms has a fireplace as its highlight. The breakfast room, kitchen, powder room, and laundry room are arranged for maximum efficiency. The second floor houses the family bedrooms. Take special note of the spacious aster suite, which features a fireplace, a splendid bath with a dressing area, and a separate lounge room.

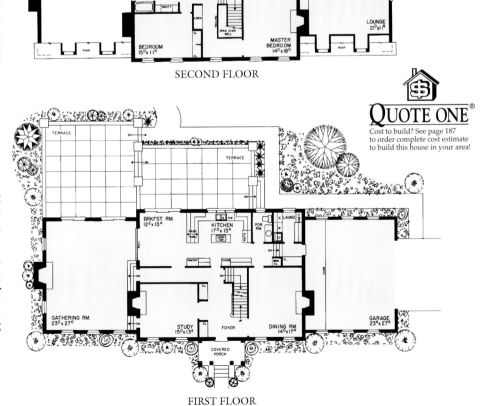

SECOND FLOOR

FIRST FLOOR

QUOTE ONE®
Cost to build? See page 187
to order complete cost estimate
to build this house in your area!

plan # HPT9700080

STYLE: NORMAN
FIRST FLOOR: 2,461 SQ. FT.
SECOND FLOOR: 1,114 SQ. FT.
TOTAL: 3,575 SQ. FT.
BEDROOMS: 4
BATHROOMS: 3½
WIDTH: 84' - 4"
DEPTH: 63' - 0"
FOUNDATION: WALKOUT
BASEMENT

SEARCH ONLINE @ EPLANS.COM

A myriad of glass and ornamental stucco detailing complements the asymmetrical facade of this two-story home. Inside, the striking two-story foyer provides a dramatic entrance. To the right is the formal dining room. An efficient L-shaped kitchen and bayed breakfast nook are conveniently located near the dining area. The living room, with its welcoming fireplace, opens through double doors to the rear terrace. The private master suite provides access to the rear terrace and adjacent study. The master bath is sure to please with its relaxing garden tub, separate shower, grand His and Hers walk-in closets, and a compartmented toilet. The second floor contains three large bedrooms, one with a private bath, while the others share a bath.

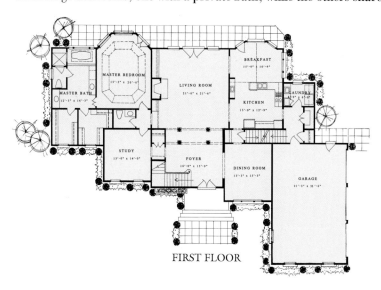

FIRST FLOOR

SECOND FLOOR

plan# HPT9700081

STYLE: EUROPEAN COTTAGE
FIRST FLOOR: 1,786 SQ. FT.
SECOND FLOOR: 1,739 SQ. FT.
TOTAL: 3,525 SQ. FT.
BEDROOMS: 5
BATHROOMS: 4½
WIDTH: 59' - 0"
DEPTH: 53' - 0"
FOUNDATION: CRAWLSPACE,
BASEMENT, SLAB

SEARCH ONLINE @ EPLANS.COM

European details bring charm and a touch of joie de vivre to this traditional home. Casual living space includes a two-story family room with a centered fireplace. A sizable kitchen, with an island serving bar and a French door to the rear property, leads to the formal dining room through a convenient butler's pantry. The second floor includes a generous master suite with a sitting room defined by decorative columns and five lovely windows. Bedroom 2 has a private bath, and two additional bedrooms share a hall bath with compartmented vanities.

SECOND FLOOR

FIRST FLOOR

plan# **HPT9700082**

STYLE: NORMAN
FIRST FLOOR: 2,639 SQ. FT.
SECOND FLOOR: 1,625 SQ. FT.
TOTAL: 4,264 SQ. FT.
BEDROOMS: 4
BATHROOMS: 3½
WIDTH: 73' - 8"
DEPTH: 58' - 6"
FOUNDATION: SLAB,
CRAWLSPACE, BASEMENT

SEARCH ONLINE @ EPLANS.COM

This home offers both luxury and practicality. A study and dining room flank the foyer, and the great room offers a warming fireplace and double French-door access to the rear yard. A butler's pantry acts as a helpful buffer between the kitchen and the columned dining room. Double bays at the rear of the home form the keeping room and the breakfast room on one side and the master bedroom on the other; note the bayed sitting area and magnificent bath in the master retreat. Three family bedrooms and two baths grace the second floor. A game room is perfect for casual family time.

FIRST FLOOR

SECOND FLOOR

COPYRIGHT LARRY E. BELK

plan # HPT9700083

STYLE: FRENCH
FIRST FLOOR: 2,608 SQ. FT.
SECOND FLOOR: 1,432 SQ. FT.
TOTAL: 4,040 SQ. FT.
BEDROOMS: 4
BATHROOMS: 3½
WIDTH: 89' - 10"
DEPTH: 63' - 8"
FOUNDATION: CRAWLSPACE,
SLAB

SEARCH ONLINE @ EPLANS.COM

A distinctively French flair is the hallmark of this European design. Inside, the two-story foyer provides views to the huge great room beyond. A well-placed study off the foyer provides space for a home office. The kitchen, breakfast room, and sunroom are adjacent to lend a spacious feel. The great room is visible from this area through decorative arches. The master suite includes a roomy sitting area and a lovely bath with a centerpiece whirlpool tub flanked by half-columns. Upstairs, Bedrooms 2 and 3 share a bath that includes separate dressing areas.

SECOND FLOOR

FIRST FLOOR

The European character of this home is enhanced through the use of stucco and stone on the exterior, giving this French Country estate home its charm and beauty. The foyer leads to the dining room and study/living room. The two-story family room is positioned for convenient access to the back staircase, kitchen, wet bar, and deck area. The master bedroom is privately located on the right side of the home with an optional entry to the study and a large garden bath. Upstairs are three additional large bedrooms; two have a shared bath and private vanities and one has a full private bath.

plan# HPT9700084

STYLE: FRENCH
FIRST FLOOR: 2,346 SQ. FT.
SECOND FLOOR: 1,260 SQ. FT.
TOTAL: 3,606 SQ. FT.
BEDROOMS: 4
BATHROOMS: 3½
WIDTH: 68' - 11"
DEPTH: 58' - 9"
FOUNDATION: WALKOUT BASEMENT

SEARCH ONLINE @ EPLANS.COM

FIRST FLOOR

SECOND FLOOR

plan# HPT9700085

STYLE: FRENCH COUNTRY
FIRST FLOOR: 2,844 SQ. FT.
SECOND FLOOR: 1,443 SQ. FT.
TOTAL: 4,287 SQ. FT.
BONUS SPACE: 360 SQ. FT.
BEDROOMS: 4
BATHROOMS: 4½
WIDTH: 72' - 0"
DEPTH: 78' - 6"
FOUNDATION: WALKOUT
BASEMENT

SEARCH ONLINE @ EPLANS.COM

This magnificent home captures the charm of French Country design with its high hipped roof and brick detailing. Inside, the two-story foyer leads directly to the spacious great room with a fireplace and three sets of double doors to the rear porch. The formal dining room sits to the left of the foyer and is near the L-shaped kitchen, which serves a bright breakfast room. The main-floor master suite takes up the entire right wing of the house and includes a large sitting area with porch access and an opulent bath. Upstairs, a gallery hall leads to a media room, three more bedrooms (each with a private bath), and a bonus room over the garage.

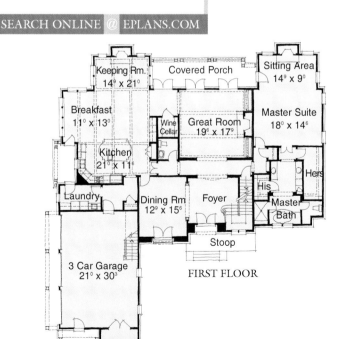

FIRST FLOOR

SECOND FLOOR

A curved wall of windows leads to the entrance of this fine home. The lavish master suite features two walk-in closets, a deluxe bath with a separate tub and shower and two vanities, a separate lounge, and an exercise room. On the other end of the home, find the highly efficient kitchen, a spacious gathering room, a round morning room and study, and a quiet guest suite. The second level is equally deluxe with two suites, a recreation room, a quiet den, and a large open area called the captain's quarters that opens to an evening deck.

plan# HPT9700086

STYLE: MEDITERRANEAN
FIRST FLOOR: 3,329 SQ. FT.
SECOND FLOOR: 1,485 SQ. FT.
TOTAL: 4,814 SQ. FT.
BEDROOMS: 4
BATHROOMS: 4½
WIDTH: 106' - 6"
DEPTH: 89' - 10"
FOUNDATION: CRAWLSPACE

SEARCH ONLINE @ EPLANS.COM

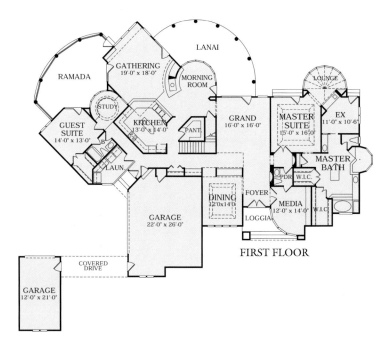

FIRST FLOOR

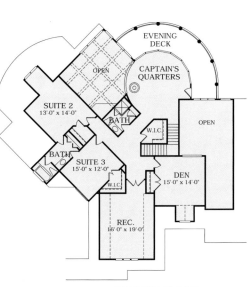

SECOND FLOOR

plan # HPT9700087

STYLE: FRENCH COUNTRY
FIRST FLOOR: 5,394 SQ. FT.
SECOND FLOOR: 1,305 SQ. FT.
TOTAL: 6,699 SQ. FT.
BEDROOMS: 5
BATHROOMS: 3½ + ½
WIDTH: 124' - 10"
DEPTH: 83' - 2"
FOUNDATION: CRAWLSPACE

SEARCH ONLINE @ EPLANS.COM

This elegant French Country estate features a plush world of luxury within. A beautiful curved staircase cascades into the welcoming foyer, which is flanked by a formal living room and the dining room with a fireplace. A butler's pantry leads to the island kitchen, which is efficiently enhanced by a walk-in storage pantry. The kitchen easily serves the breakfast room. The covered rear porch is accessed from the media/family room and the great room warmed by a fireplace. The master suite is a sumptuous retreat highlighted by its lavish bath and two huge walk-in closets. Next door, double doors open to a large study. All family bedrooms feature walk-in closets. Bedrooms 2 and 3 share a bath. Upstairs, Bedrooms 4 and 5 share another hall bath. A home office is located above the three-car garage.

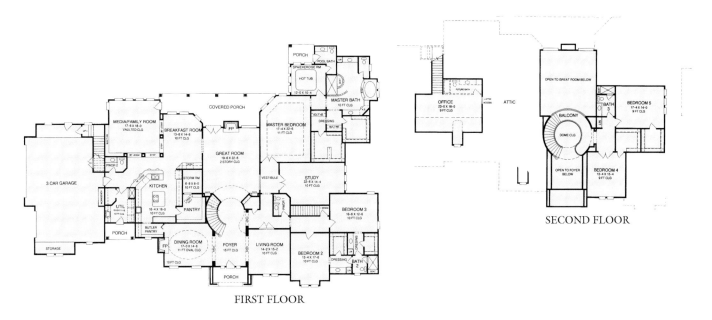

FIRST FLOOR

SECOND FLOOR

plan# HPT9700088

STYLE: COUNTRY COTTAGE
FIRST FLOOR: 2,060 SQ. FT.
SECOND FLOOR: 1,817 SQ. FT.
TOTAL: 3,877 SQ. FT.
BEDROOMS: 5
BATHROOMS: 4½
WIDTH: 54' - 0"
DEPTH: 78' - 4"
FOUNDATION: CRAWLSPACE,
BASEMENT, SLAB

SEARCH ONLINE @ EPLANS.COM

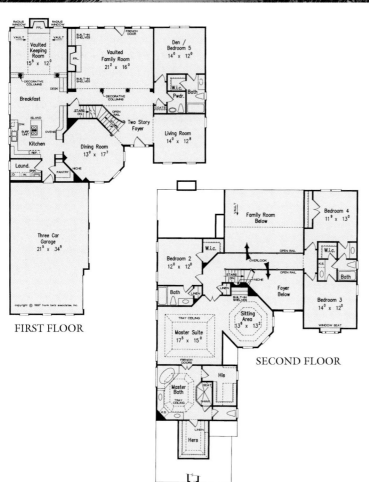

FIRST FLOOR

SECOND FLOOR

Mesmerizing details make this luxurious home a distinct sensation. Stucco and stone, opulent arches, and French shutters romanticize the exterior. Inside, a sweeping staircase cascades into the two-story foyer. The eye-catching stone turret encloses the dining room. The formal living room is illuminated by two enormous arched windows. A wall of windows in the family room offers a breathtaking view of the backyard. The island kitchen adjoins the breakfast area and a walk-in pantry. A three-car garage completes the ground level. Upstairs, the master wing is almost doubled by its private sitting area. Double doors open into the master bath with a corner whirlpool tub. Enormous His and Hers walk-in closets are efficiently designed.

plan# HPT9700089

STYLE: PLANTATION
FIRST FLOOR: 2,113 SQ. FT.
SECOND FLOOR: 2,098 SQ. FT.
TOTAL: 4,211 SQ. FT.
BEDROOMS: 5
BATHROOMS: 4½
WIDTH: 68' - 6"
DEPTH: 53' - 0"
FOUNDATION: SLAB,
CRAWLSPACE, BASEMENT

SEARCH ONLINE @ EPLANS.COM

This two-story farmhouse has much to offer, with the most exciting feature being the opulent master suite, which takes up almost the entire width of the upper level. French doors access the large master bedroom with its coffered ceiling. Steps lead to a separate sitting room with a fireplace and sun-filled bay window. His and Hers walk-in closets lead the way to a vaulted private bath with separate vanities and a lavish whirlpool tub. On the first floor, an island kitchen and a bayed breakfast room flow into a two-story family room with a raised-hearth fireplace, built-in shelves, and French-door access to the rear yard.

SECOND FLOOR

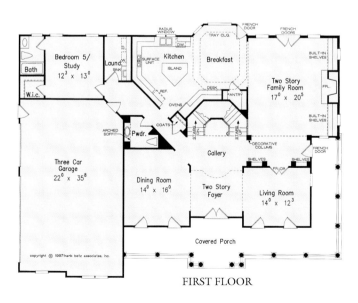

FIRST FLOOR

plan# HPT9700090

STYLE: COUNTRY COTTAGE
FIRST FLOOR: 3,248 SQ. FT.
SECOND FLOOR: 1,426 SQ. FT.
TOTAL: 4,674 SQ. FT.
BEDROOMS: 5
BATHROOMS: 5½ + ½
WIDTH: 99' - 10"
DEPTH: 74' - 10"
FOUNDATION: BASEMENT

SEARCH ONLINE @ EPLANS.COM

Multiple rooflines; a stone, brick, and siding facade; and an absolutely grand entrance combine to give this home the look of luxury. A striking family room showcases a beautiful fireplace framed with built-ins. The nearby breakfast room streams with light and accesses the rear patio. The kitchen features an island workstation, walk-in pantry, and plenty of counter space. A guest suite is available on the first floor, perfect for when family members visit. The first-floor master suite enjoys easy access to a large study, bayed sitting room, and luxurious bath. Private baths are also included for each of the upstairs bedrooms.

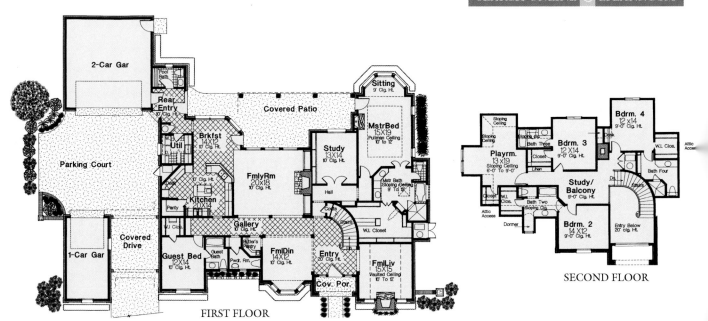

FIRST FLOOR

SECOND FLOOR

plan# HPT9700091

STYLE: TRADITIONAL
FIRST FLOOR: 2,814 SQ. FT.
SECOND FLOOR: 979 SQ. FT.
TOTAL: 3,793 SQ. FT.
BEDROOMS: 4
BATHROOMS: 3½
WIDTH: 98' - 0"
DEPTH: 45' - 10"
FOUNDATION: SLAB, BASEMENT

SEARCH ONLINE @ EPLANS.COM

A covered, columned porch and symmetrically placed windows welcome you to this elegant brick home. The formal living room offers built-in bookshelves and one of two fireplaces, the other being found in the spacious family room. A gallery running between these rooms leads to the sumptuous master suite, which includes a sitting area, a private covered patio, and a bath with two walk-in closets, dual vanities, a large shower, and a garden tub. The step-saving kitchen features a work island and a snack bar. The breakfast and family rooms offer doors to the large covered veranda. Upstairs you'll find three bedrooms and attic storage space. The three-car garage even has room for a golf cart.

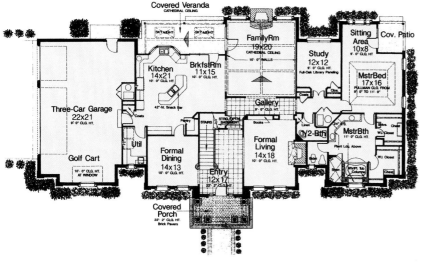

FIRST FLOOR

SECOND FLOOR

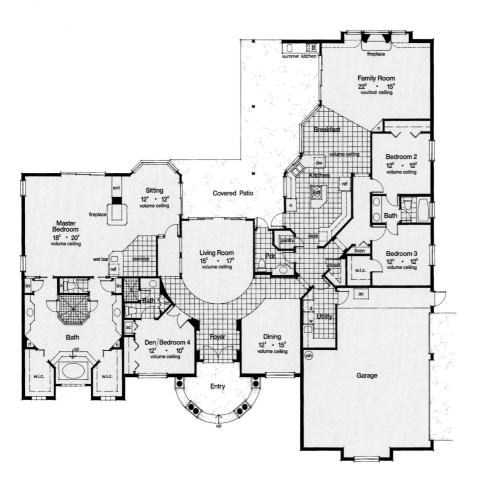

plan# HPT9700092

STYLE: CONTEMPORARY
SQUARE FOOTAGE: 3,556
BEDROOMS: 4
BATHROOMS: 3½
WIDTH: 85' - 0"
DEPTH: 85' - 0"
FOUNDATION: SLAB

SEARCH ONLINE @ EPLANS.COM

A beautiful curved portico provides a majestic entrance to this one-story home. To the left of the foyer is a den/bedroom with a private bath, ideal for use as a guest suite. The exquisite master suite features a see-through fireplace and an exercise area with a wet bar. The family wing is geared for casual living with a powder room/patio bath, a huge island kitchen with a walk-in pantry, a glass-walled breakfast nook, and a grand family room with a fireplace and media wall. Two family bedrooms share a private bath.

plan# HPT9700093

L

STYLE: FLORIDIAN
SQUARE FOOTAGE: 4,565
BEDROOMS: 3
BATHROOMS: 3½
WIDTH: 88'-0"
DEPTH: 95'-0"
FOUNDATION: SLAB

SEARCH ONLINE @ EPLANS.COM

A freestanding entryway is the focal point of this luxurious residence. It has an arch motif that is carried through to the rear using a gabled roof and a vaulted ceiling from the foyer out to the lanai. The kitchen, which features a cooktop island and plenty of counter space, opens to the leisure area with a handy snack bar. Two guest suites with private baths are just off this casual living space. The master wing is truly pampering, stretching the entire length of the home. The suite has a large sitting area, a corner fireplace, and a morning kitchen. The bath features an island vanity, a raised tub with a curved glass wall overlooking a private garden, a sauna, and separate closets. An exercise room has a curved glass wall and a pocket door to the study, where a wet bar is ready to serve refreshments.

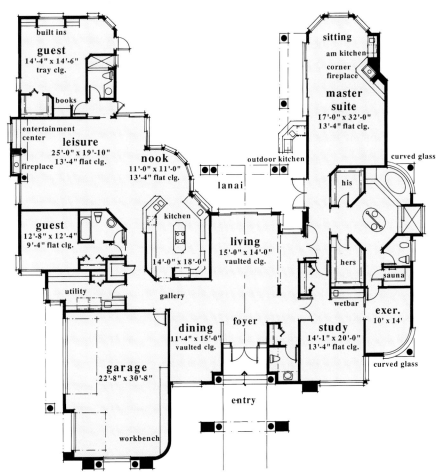

plan# **HPT9700094**

STYLE: MEDITERRANEAN
SQUARE FOOTAGE: 4,222
BONUS SPACE: 590 SQ. FT.
BEDROOMS: 4
BATHROOMS: 5
WIDTH: 83' - 10"
DEPTH: 112' - 0"
FOUNDATION: SLAB

SEARCH ONLINE @ EPLANS.COM

The striking facade of this magnificent estate is just the beginning of the excitement you will encounter inside. The foyer passes the formal dining room on the way to the columned gallery. The formal living room opens to the rear patio and has easy access to a wet bar. The contemporary kitchen has a work island and all the amenities for gourmet preparation. The family room will be a favorite for casual entertainment. The family sleeping wing begins with an octagonal vestibule and has three bedrooms with private baths. The master wing features a private garden and an opulent bath.

plan# HPT9700095

STYLE: MEDITERRANEAN
FIRST FLOOR: 3,568 SQ. FT.
SECOND FLOOR: 1,667 SQ. FT.
TOTAL: 5,235 SQ. FT.
BEDROOMS: 4
BATHROOMS: 3½
WIDTH: 86' - 8"
DEPTH: 79' - 0"
FOUNDATION: WALKOUT
BASEMENT

SEARCH ONLINE @ EPLANS.COM

The ornamental stucco detailing on this home creates an Old World charm. The two-story foyer with a sweeping curved stair opens to the large formal dining room and study. The two-story great room overlooks the rear patio. A large kitchen with an island workstation opens to an octagonal-shaped breakfast room and the family room. The master suite, offering convenient access to the study, is complete with a fireplace, two walk-in closets, and a bath with twin vanities and a separate shower and tub. A staircase located off the family room provides additional access to the three second-floor bedrooms that all offer walk-in closets and plenty of storage.

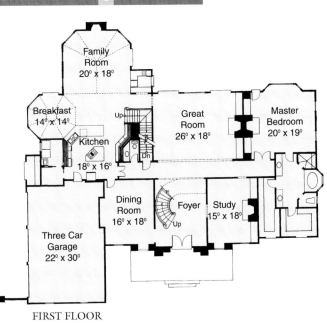

FIRST FLOOR

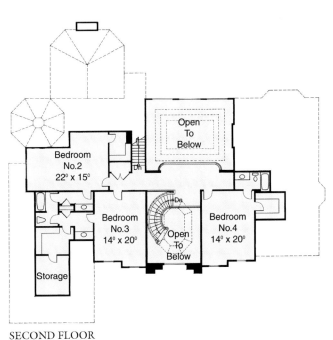

SECOND FLOOR

plan# **HPT9700096**

STYLE: MEDITERRANEAN
FIRST FLOOR: 4,323 SQ. FT.
SECOND FLOOR: 2,226 SQ. FT.
TOTAL: 6,549 SQ. FT.
BONUS SPACE: 453 SQ. FT.
BEDROOMS: 5
BATHROOMS: 5½ + ½
WIDTH: 98' - 8"
DEPTH: 102' - 8"
FOUNDATION: SLAB

SEARCH ONLINE @ EPLANS.COM

This Italian Renaissance marvel has it all—five bedrooms, a game room, a theater, and expansive areas for formal parties and relaxed barbecues. A covered patio winds around the entire rear of the home, and a sundeck is located on the second level. A wet bar and circular balcony, with an outside spiral stairway, make the upstairs game room a great party site. The lavish master suite features a circular sitting area with windows drawing in natural light from many directions. A spiral stairway winds gracefully upstairs from the impressive main-floor entry, or, if you prefer, take the elevator. A semicircular turret on the corner of the three-car garage is not only flashy, it is a handy storage area.

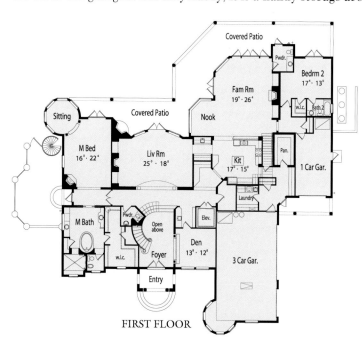

FIRST FLOOR

SECOND FLOOR

plan# HPT9700097

STYLE: MEDITERRANEAN
FIRST FLOOR: 2,926 SQ. FT.
SECOND FLOOR: 1,268 SQ. FT.
TOTAL: 4,194 SQ. FT.
BONUS SPACE: 353 SQ. FT.
BEDROOMS: 4
BATHROOMS: 4½
WIDTH: 75' - 0"
DEPTH: 85' - 4"
FOUNDATION: SLAB

SEARCH ONLINE @ EPLANS.COM

This magnificent Mediterranean-style home is full of the charms that make entertaining gracious and family life comfortable. From the elegant covered entry, pass into the foyer or, through separate French doors, into the den on the right and the formal dining room on the left. A superb kitchen, sunlit breakfast nook, and family room flow together, creating a relaxed unit. Splendor awaits in the master suite with its gracefully curved bedchamber, huge walk-in wardrobes, and luxuriant bath. On the opposite side of the house, a guest bedroom enjoys a full bath. Two more bedrooms share a bath on the second level, and additional space is available for another bedroom and bath. The rear covered patio can be entered from the living room, the master suite, or the breakfast nook. Three vehicles will easily fit into the side-loading garage.

FIRST FLOOR

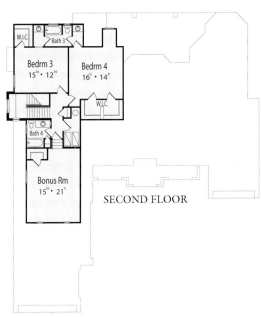

SECOND FLOOR

plan# HPT9700098

STYLE: MEDITERRANEAN
MAIN LEVEL: 2,959 SQ. FT.
UPPER LEVEL: 1,055 SQ. FT.
LOWER LEVEL: 1,270 SQ. FT.
TOTAL: 5,284 SQ. FT.
BEDROOMS: 4
BATHROOMS: 5½
WIDTH: 110' - 4"
DEPTH: 72' - 5"
FOUNDATION: SLAB, BASEMENT

SEARCH ONLINE @ EPLANS.COM

UPPER LEVEL

MAIN LEVEL

LOWER LEVEL

Designed for a sloping lot, this fantastic Mediterranean home features all the views to the rear, making it the perfect home for an ocean, lake, or golf-course view. Inside, the great room features a rear wall of windows. The breakfast room, kitchen, dining room, and master suite also feature rear views. A three-level series of porches is located on the back for outdoor relaxing. The master suite boasts a large sitting area, resplendent bath, and access to a private porch. Two bedroom suites are found upstairs, each with a private bath and a porch. The basement of this home features another bedroom suite and a large game room. An expandable area can be used as an office or Bedroom 5.

plan# HPT9700099

STYLE: FRENCH
FIRST FLOOR: 2,899 SQ. FT.
SECOND FLOOR: 1,472 SQ. FT.
TOTAL: 4,371 SQ. FT.
BEDROOMS: 4
BATHROOMS: 3½
WIDTH: 69' - 4"
DEPTH: 76' - 8"
FOUNDATION: SLAB

SEARCH ONLINE @ EPLANS.COM

Finished with French Country adornments, this estate home is comfortable in just about any setting. Main living areas are sunk down just a bit from the entry, providing them with soaring ceilings and sweeping views. The family room features a focal fireplace. A columned entry gains access to the master suite where separate sitting and sleeping areas are defined by a three-sided fireplace. There are three bedrooms upstairs; one has a private bath. The sunken media room on this level includes storage space. Look for the decks on the second level.

FIRST FLOOR

SECOND FLOOR

OPTIONAL LAYOUT

plan# HPT9700100

STYLE: TRADITIONAL
FIRST FLOOR: 2,813 SQ. FT.
SECOND FLOOR: 1,091 SQ. FT.
TOTAL: 3,904 SQ. FT.
BEDROOMS: 4
BATHROOMS: 3½
WIDTH: 85' - 5"
DEPTH: 74' - 8"

SEARCH ONLINE @ EPLANS.COM

Keystone lintels and an arched transom over the entry spell classic design for this four-bedroom home. The tiled foyer offers entry to any room you choose, whether it's the secluded den with its built-in bookshelves, the formal dining room, the formal living room with its fireplace, or the spacious rear family room and kitchen area with a sunny breakfast nook. The first-floor master suite features a sitting room with book-shelves, two walk-in closets, and a private bath with a corner whirlpool tub. Upstairs, two family bedrooms share a bath and enjoy separate vanities. A third family bed-room features its own full bath and a built-in window seat in a box-bay window.

FIRST FLOOR

SECOND FLOOR

plan# HPT9700101

STYLE: TRADITIONAL
FIRST FLOOR: 2,603 SQ. FT.
SECOND FLOOR: 1,020 SQ. FT.
TOTAL: 3,623 SQ. FT.
BEDROOMS: 4
BATHROOMS: 4½
WIDTH: 76' - 8"
DEPTH: 68' - 0"

SEARCH ONLINE @ EPLANS.COM

Perhaps the most notable characteristic of this traditional house is its masterful use of space. The glorious great room, open dining room, and handsome den serve as the heart of the home. A cozy hearth room with a fireplace rounds out the kitchen and breakfast area. The master bedroom opens up to a private sitting room with a fireplace. Three family bedrooms occupy the second floor, each one with a private bath. Other special features include a four-car garage, a corner whirlpool tub in the master bath, a walk-in pantry and snack bar in the kitchen, and transom windows in the dining room.

QUOTE ONE®

Cost to build? See page 187 to order complete cost estimate to build this house in your area!

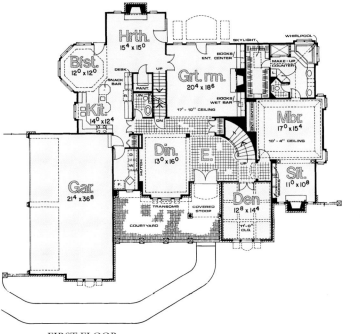

FIRST FLOOR

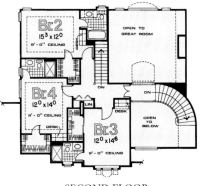

SECOND FLOOR

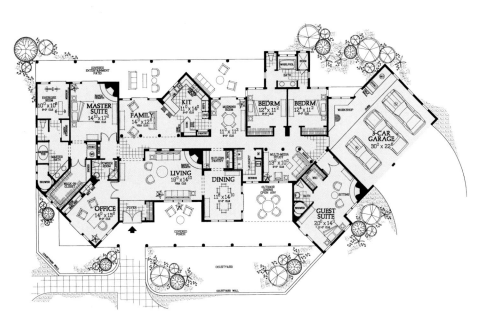

plan# HPT9700102

STYLE: SW CONTEMPORARY
SQUARE FOOTAGE: 3,838
BEDROOMS: 4
BATHROOMS: 3½
WIDTH: 127' - 6"
DEPTH: 60' - 10"
FOUNDATION: SLAB

SEARCH ONLINE @ EPLANS.COM

This diamond in the desert gives new meaning to old style. A courtyard leads to a covered porch with nooks for sitting and open-air dining. The gracious living room is highlighted by a corner fireplace; the formal dining room comes with an adjacent butler's pantry and access to the porch dining area. Two sleeping zones are luxurious with whirlpool tubs and separate showers. The master suite also boasts an exercise room and a nearby private office. A guest suite includes a private entrance and another corner fireplace.

QUOTE ONE®

Cost to build? See page 187
to order complete cost estimate
to build this house in your area!

OPULENT BATHS

plan # HPT9700103

STYLE: GREEK REVIVAL
FIRST FLOOR: 3,509 SQ. FT.
SECOND FLOOR: 1,564 SQ. FT.
TOTAL: 5,073 SQ. FT.
BEDROOMS: 4
BATHROOMS: 4½ + ½
WIDTH: 86' - 6"
DEPTH: 67' - 3"
FOUNDATION: WALKOUT
BASEMENT

SEARCH ONLINE @ EPLANS.COM

Classic symmetry sets off this graceful exterior, with two sets of double columns framed by tall windows and topped with a detailed pediment. Just off the foyer, the study and dining room present an elegant impression. The gourmet kitchen offers a food-preparation island and a lovely breakfast bay. The central gallery hall connects casual living areas with the master wing. A delightful dressing area with a split vanity and a bay window indulges the lavish master bath, which boasts a walk-in shower and compartmented toilet. The master bedroom features a bumped-out glass sitting area, a tray ceiling, and a romantic fireplace. Upstairs, three bedroom suites are pampered with private baths.

FIRST FLOOR

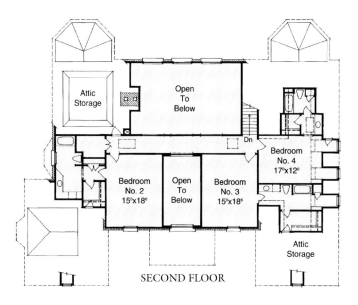

SECOND FLOOR

plan# HPT9700104

STYLE: PLANTATION
FIRST FLOOR: 2,913 SQ. FT.
SECOND FLOOR: 1,380 SQ. FT.
TOTAL: 4,293 SQ. FT.
BONUS SPACE: 905 SQ. FT.
BEDROOMS: 4
BATHROOMS: 4½
WIDTH: 88' - 4"
DEPTH: 100' - 8"
FOUNDATION: CRAWLSPACE

SEARCH ONLINE @ EPLANS.COM

Sturdy columns and a widow's walk add Colonial flair to this imposing Plantation-style design. Four fireplaces—in the dining room, library, family room, and master bedroom—add warmth and grandeur to the first floor. Other special amenities include a wealth of built-ins—seats and bookcases in the library, an entertainment center in the family room, and shelves in the master-suite closet—walk-in closets and private baths for all the secondary bedrooms, and a large upstairs sewing room. The upper porch, with a distinctive wrought-iron handrail, is accessible from the upstairs hallway.

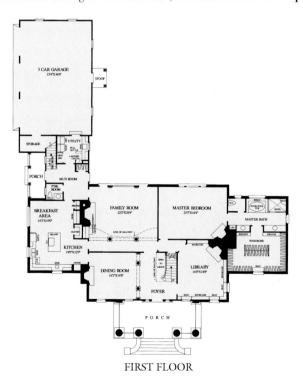

FIRST FLOOR

SECOND FLOOR

plan# HPT9700105

STYLE: GREEK REVIVAL
FIRST FLOOR: 3,902 SQ. FT.
SECOND FLOOR: 2,159 SQ. FT.
TOTAL: 6,061 SQ. FT.
BEDROOMS: 5
BATHROOMS: 3½
WIDTH: 85' - 3"
DEPTH: 74' - 0"
FOUNDATION: WALKOUT
BASEMENT

SEARCH ONLINE @ EPLANS.COM

The entry to this classic home is framed with a sweeping double staircase and four large columns topped with a pediment. The two-story foyer is flanked by spacious living and dining rooms. The two-story family room, which has a central fireplace, opens to the study and a solarium. A spacious U-shaped kitchen features a central island cooktop. An additional staircase off the breakfast room offers convenient access to the second floor. The impressive master suite features backyard access and a bath fit for royalty, with two vanities, a garden tub set in a bay window, and a compartmented toilet. Four bedrooms upstairs enjoy large proportions.

FIRST FLOOR

SECOND FLOOR

plan# HPT9700106

STYLE: EUROPEAN COTTAGE
FIRST FLOOR: 2,995 SQ. FT.
SECOND FLOOR: 1,102 SQ. FT.
TOTAL: 4,097 SQ. FT.
BEDROOMS: 4
BATHROOMS: 3½
WIDTH: 120' - 6"
DEPTH: 58' - 8"
FOUNDATION: SLAB

SEARCH ONLINE @ EPLANS.COM

This enchanting chateau sings of refined European luxury. A formal dining room and study flank the entry. A massive stone fireplace warms the great room, which provides a wall of glass with views to the covered patio and beyond to the rear property. Casual areas include the kitchen, breakfast, and recreation rooms. A deluxe tiled kitchen provides a snack counter that overlooks a beautiful morning nook. The master bedroom, with a bayed sitting area, boasts a luxurious bath with a Pullman ceiling and two walk-in closets. Three addtional bedrooms are located upstairs.

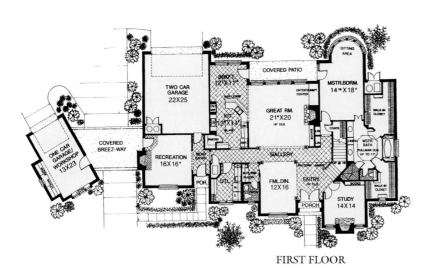

FIRST FLOOR

SECOND FLOOR

plan# HPT9700107

STYLE: TRADITIONAL
FIRST FLOOR: 2,751 SQ. FT.
SECOND FLOOR: 1,185 SQ. FT.
TOTAL: 3,936 SQ. FT.
BONUS SPACE: 289 SQ. FT.
BEDROOMS: 4
BATHROOMS: 3½
WIDTH: 79' - 0"
DEPTH: 66' - 4"
FOUNDATION: SLAB, BASEMENT

SEARCH ONLINE @ EPLANS.COM

This grand brick home boasts muntin windows, multilevel rooflines, cut-brick jack arches, and a beautifully arched entry. A cathedral-ceilinged living room, complete with a fireplace, and a family dining room flank the 20-foot high entry. Relax in the family room, mix a drink from the wet bar, and look out through multiple windows to the covered veranda. A luxurious master suite includes a windowed sitting area looking over the rear view, private patio, walk-in closet, and a full bath boasting a 10-foot ceiling, separate shower, and compartmented toilet. On the second level, the three high-ceilinged bedrooms share two full baths and a study area with a built-in desk.

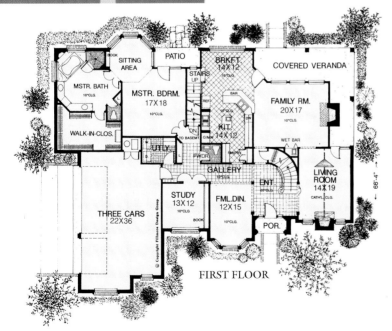

FIRST FLOOR

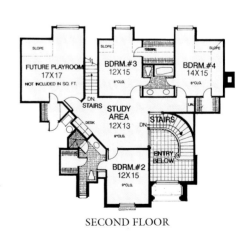

SECOND FLOOR

plan# HPT9700108

STYLE: FRENCH
FIRST FLOOR: 3,168 SQ. FT.
SECOND FLOOR: 998 SQ. FT.
TOTAL: 4,166 SQ. FT.
BONUS SPACE: 210 SQ. FT.
BEDROOMS: 4
BATHROOMS: 3½
WIDTH: 90' - 0"
DEPTH: 63' - 5"
FOUNDATION: SLAB,
BASEMENT, CRAWLSPACE

SEARCH ONLINE @ EPLANS.COM

Stucco corner quoins, multiple gables, and graceful columns all combine to give this European manor plenty of appeal. Inside, a gallery entry presents a formal dining room on the right, defined by elegant columns, while the formal living room awaits just ahead. The highly efficient kitchen features a worktop island, pantry, and a serving bar to the nearby octagonal breakfast area. The family room offers a built-in entertainment center, a fireplace, and its own covered patio. The left side of the first floor is dedicated to the master suite. Here, the homeowner is pampered with an octagonal study, a huge walk-in closet, a lavish bath with a dual-sink vanity and compartmented toilet, and a convenient nursery. The second floor contains two family bedrooms, each with a walk-in closet, and a media area with built-in bookshelves.

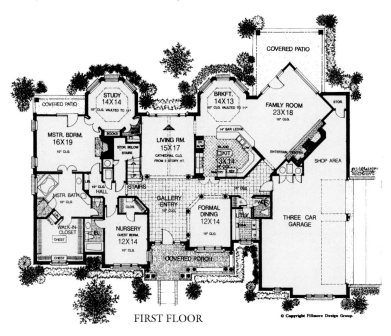

FIRST FLOOR

SECOND FLOOR

plan# HPT9700109

STYLE: GEORGIAN
FIRST FLOOR: 3,599 SQ. FT.
SECOND FLOOR: 1,621 SQ. FT.
TOTAL: 5,220 SQ. FT.
BONUS SPACE: 356 SQ. FT.
BEDROOMS: 4
BATHROOMS: 5½
WIDTH: 108' - 10"
DEPTH: 53' - 10"
FOUNDATION: SLAB, BASEMENT

SEARCH ONLINE @ EPLANS.COM

A grand facade detailed with brick corner quoins, stucco flourishes, arched windows, and an elegant entrance presents this home. A spacious foyer is accented by curving stairs and flanked by a formal living room and a formal dining room. For cozy times, a through-fireplace is located between a large family room and a quiet study. The master bedroom is designed to pamper, with two walk-in closets, a two-sided fireplace, a bayed sitting area, and an opulent private bath with a linen closet, whirlpool tub, and walk-in shower. Upstairs, three secondary bedrooms each have a private bath and walk-in closet. Also on this level is a spacious recreation room, perfect for a game room or children's playroom.

FIRST FLOOR

SECOND FLOOR

© The Sater Design Collection, Inc.

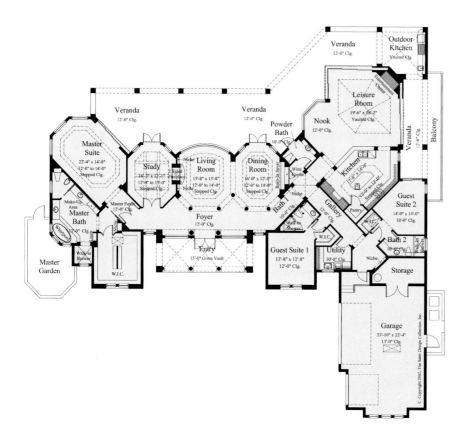

plan# HPT9700110

STYLE: EUROPEAN COTTAGE
SQUARE FOOTAGE: 3,640
BEDROOMS: 3
BATHROOMS: 3½
WIDTH: 106' - 4"
DEPTH: 102' - 4"
FOUNDATION: SLAB

SEARCH ONLINE @ EPLANS.COM

Come home to luxurious living—all on one level—with this striking Mediterranean plan. Unique ceiling treatments highlight the living areas—the living and dining rooms, as well as the study, feature stepped ceilings, while the leisure room soars with a vaulted ceiling. The gourmet kitchen includes a spacious center island; another kitchen, this one outdoors, can be accessed from the leisure room. The master suite boasts plenty of amenities: a large, skylit walk-in closet, a bath with a whirlpool tub and walk-in shower, and private access to a charming garden area. Two suites, both with private baths, sit to the right of the plan.

plan# HPT9700111

STYLE: TRADITIONAL
FIRST FLOOR: 3,546 SQ. FT.
SECOND FLOOR: 1,213 SQ. FT.
TOTAL: 4,759 SQ. FT.
BEDROOMS: 4
BATHROOMS: 3½
WIDTH: 96' - 0"
DEPTH: 83' - 0"
FOUNDATION: BASEMENT

SEARCH ONLINE @ EPLANS.COM

A marvelous arched entry welcomes you to call this beautiful mansion home. Inside, the two-story foyer leads under the second floor balcony into the lavish living room, which is graced by a through-fireplace to the study and three sets of double French doors to the rear terrace. A huge octagonal leisure room at the back of the plan offers a built-in entertainment center. A large kitchen with a cooktop island easily serves both the formal dining room and the sunny breakfast nook. The master suite, located at the far right of the plan, is lit from the bay window and has access to a rear veranda. Large His and Hers walk-in closets will fulfill all your storage needs and a sumptuous private bath, with two vanities and a bay window, is designed to pamper. Upstairs, three family bedrooms each have a walk-in closet.

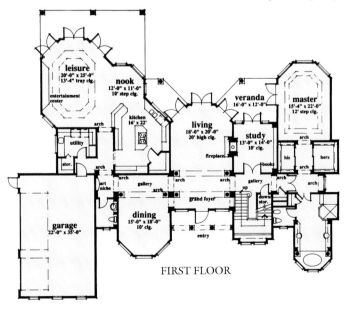

FIRST FLOOR

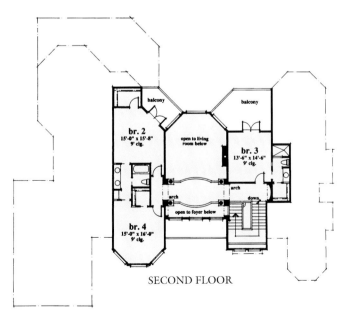

SECOND FLOOR

This luxury home hosts over 1,000 square feet of outdoor living space, including private balconies on two of the bedrooms. Although the Mediterranean-inspired facade of this home will be the envy of your neighborhood, the true glory of the design is the brilliant floor plan inside. The foyer ushers guests into a bayed living room with three sets of French doors. A two-way fireplace shared with the study is a cozy touch. A vast country kitchen effortlessly serves the elegant dining room and cheerful nook. A rear leisure room is awash with light, making it the perfect place for casual relaxation. If complete pampering is what you crave, look no further than the master suite, with abundant natural light and a lavish whirlpool bath. The plan is completed by three upper-level bedrooms and a loft overlook.

plan# HPT9700112

STYLE: TRADITIONAL
FIRST FLOOR: 3,556 SQ. FT.
SECOND FLOOR: 1,308 SQ. FT.
TOTAL: 4,864 SQ. FT.
BEDROOMS: 4
BATHROOMS: 3½
WIDTH: 95' - 0"
DEPTH: 84' - 8"
FOUNDATION: SLAB

SEARCH ONLINE @ EPLANS.COM

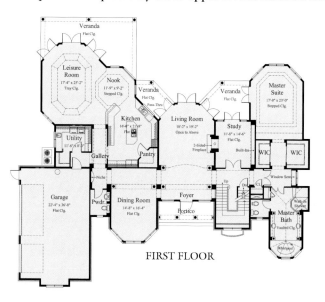

FIRST FLOOR

SECOND FLOOR

plan# HPT9700113

STYLE: EUROPEAN COTTAGE
FIRST FLOOR: 2,834 SQ. FT.
SECOND FLOOR: 1,143 SQ. FT.
TOTAL: 3,977 SQ. FT.
BEDROOMS: 4
BATHROOMS: 3½
WIDTH: 85' - 0"
DEPTH: 76' - 8"
FOUNDATION: SLAB

SEARCH ONLINE @ EPLANS.COM

Mediterranean accents enhance the facade of this contemporary estate home. Two fanciful turret bays add a sense of grandeur to the exterior. Double doors open inside to a grand two-story foyer. A two-sided fireplace warms the study and living room, with a two-story coffered ceiling. To the right, the master suite includes a private bath with a walk-in shower and whirlpool tub, two walk-in closets, and double-door access to the sweeping rear veranda. Casual areas of the home include the gourmet island kitchen, breakfast nook, and leisure room warmed by a fireplace. A spiral staircase leads upstairs, where a second-floor balcony separates two family bedrooms from the luxurious guest suite.

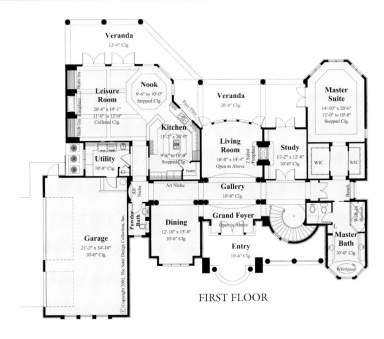

FIRST FLOOR

SECOND FLOOR

plan# HPT9700114

STYLE: TRADITIONAL
SQUARE FOOTAGE: 3,790
BEDROOMS: 4
BATHROOMS: 3½
WIDTH: 80' - 0"
DEPTH: 107' - 8"
FOUNDATION: SLAB

SEARCH ONLINE @ EPLANS.COM

OPTIONAL LAYOUT

A majestic design, this well-planned home puts family comfort and privacy first. Enter under a keystone portico to the foyer; a dramatic dining room opens to the right. Just ahead, the living room is an inviting place to relax by the fireplace under the coffered ceiling. A unique kitchen supports gourmet meals or a quick snack enjoyed in the sunny nook. An entertainment center separates the leisure room and game room—or finish the space to include a fourth bedroom. The rear guest suite offers a private bath and access to the veranda, featuring an outdoor grill. For the ultimate in luxury, the master suite is peerless; a light-filled sitting area, an angled bedroom, and an indulgent bath with a whirlpool tub and lighted make-up area make an inviting retreat for any homeowner.

© The Sater Design Collection, Inc.

plan # HPT9700115

STYLE: ITALIANATE
SQUARE FOOTAGE: 3,942
BEDROOMS: 3
BATHROOMS: 4
WIDTH: 83' - 10"
DEPTH: 106' - 0"
FOUNDATION: SLAB

SEARCH ONLINE @ EPLANS.COM

Italian Renaissance flair sets the tone for this majestic Old World estate. An impressive entrance reveals an open floor plan; the foyer, living room, and dining room are all defined by distinctive ceiling treatments for endless interior design possibilities. A wet bar and pool bath announce the gourmet kitchen with a pentagonal island and lots of counter space. Past a half-moon nook, the leisure room will be a family favorite. On the lanai, an outdoor kitchen is an easy way to cook up all-weather fun. To the far right, the master suite will amaze; an octagonal sitting area and morning kitchen are only the beginning. Two enormous walk-in closets beckon with built-in shelving and room for even the biggest clotheshorses' collections. The master bath, set in a turret, will soothe and pamper with a central whirlpool tub, walk-in shower, and views to the garden.

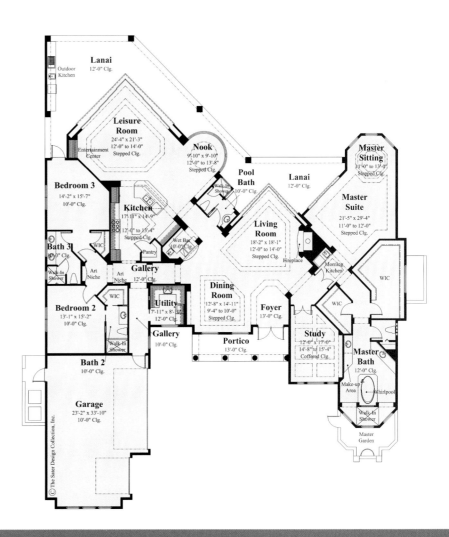

plan# HPT9700116

STYLE: ITALIANATE
FIRST FLOOR: 2,491 SQ. FT.
SECOND FLOOR: 1,290 SQ. FT.
TOTAL: 3,781 SQ. FT.
BEDROOMS: 5
BATHROOMS: 4½
WIDTH: 62' - 0"
DEPTH: 67' - 0"
FOUNDATION: BASEMENT

SEARCH ONLINE @ EPLANS.COM

Chic and glamorous, this Mediterranean facade pairs ancient shapes, such as square columns, with a refined disposition set off by radius windows. A magnificent entry leads to an interior gallery and the great room. This extraordinary space is warmed by a two-sided fireplace and defined by extended views of the rear property. Sliding glass doors to a wraparound veranda create great indoor/outdoor flow. The gourmet kitchen easily serves any occasion and provides a pass-through to the outdoor kitchen. A powder room accommodates visitors, while an elevator leads to the sleeping quarters upstairs. Double doors open to the master suite, which features a walk-in closet, two-sided fireplace, and angled whirlpool bath. The master bedroom boasts a tray ceiling and doors to a spacious deck. The upper-level catwalk leads to a bedroom suite that can easily accommodate a guest or live-in relative. The basement level features future space and a two-car garage.

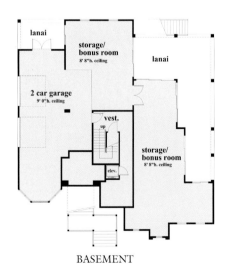

BASEMENT

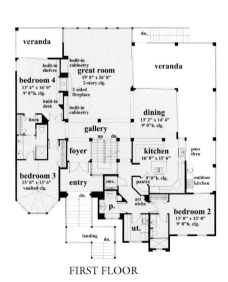

FIRST FLOOR

SECOND FLOOR

plan# HPT9700117

STYLE: MEDITERRANEAN
MAIN LEVEL: 2,391 SQ. FT.
UPPER LEVEL: 922 SQ. FT.
LOWER LEVEL: 1,964 SQ. FT.
TOTAL: 5,277 SQ. FT.
BONUS SPACE: 400 SQ. FT.
BEDROOMS: 4
BATHROOMS: 4½
WIDTH: 63' - 10"
DEPTH: 85' - 6"
FOUNDATION: BASEMENT

SEARCH ONLINE @ EPLANS.COM

Here's an upscale multilevel plan with expansive rear views. The first floor provides an open living and dining area, defined by decorative columns and enhanced by natural light from tall windows. A breakfast area with a lovely triple window opens to a sunroom, which allows light to pour into the gourmet kitchen. The master wing features a tray ceiling in the bedroom, two walk-in closets, and an elegant private vestibule leading to a lavish bath. Upstairs, a reading loft overlooks the great room and leads to a sleeping area with two suites. A recreation room, exercise room, office, guest suite, and additional storage are available in the finished basement.

LOWER LEVEL

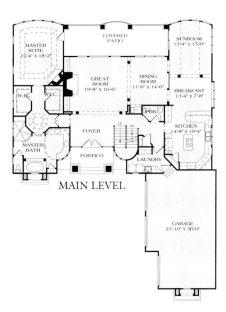

MAIN LEVEL

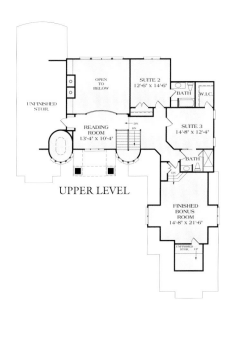

UPPER LEVEL

plan# HPT9700118

Gently curved arches and dormers contrast with the straight lines of gables and wooden columns on this French-style stone exterior. Small-paned windows are enhanced by shutters; tall chimneys and a cupola add height. Inside, a spacious gathering room with an impressive fireplace opens to a cheery morning room. The kitchen is a delight, with a beamed ceiling, triangular work island, walk-in pantry, and angular counter with a snack bar. The nearby laundry room includes a sink, a work area, and plenty of room for storage. The first-floor master suite boasts a bay-windowed sitting nook, a deluxe bath with a dual-sink vanity, garden tub, and separate shower, and a handy study.

STYLE: COUNTRY COTTAGE
FIRST FLOOR: 2,660 SQ. FT.
SECOND FLOOR: 914 SQ. FT.
TOTAL: 3,574 SQ. FT.
BONUS SPACE: 733 SQ. FT.
BEDROOMS: 3
BATHROOMS: 4½
WIDTH: 114' - 8"
DEPTH: 75' - 10"
FOUNDATION: CRAWLSPACE

SEARCH ONLINE @ EPLANS.COM

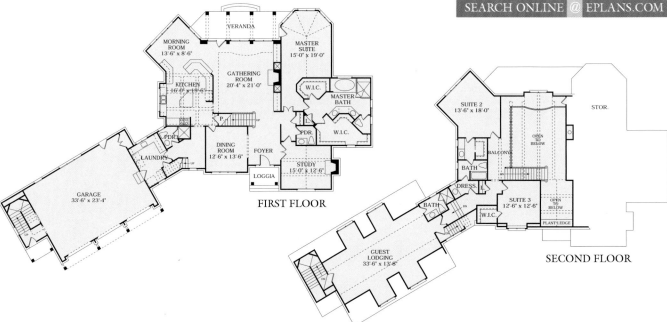

FIRST FLOOR

SECOND FLOOR

plan# HPT9700119

STYLE: TRANSITIONAL
MAIN LEVEL: 2,562 SQ. FT.
LOWER LEVEL: 1,955 SQ. FT.
TOTAL: 4,517 SQ. FT.
BEDROOMS: 3
BATHROOMS: 2½ + ½
WIDTH: 75' - 8"
DEPTH: 70' - 6"
FOUNDATION: BASEMENT

SEARCH ONLINE @ EPLANS.COM

A brick and stone exterior with a tower and recessed entry creates a strong, solid look to this enchanting home. The large foyer introduces the great room, with a beamed ceiling and tall windows for a rear view. The dining room is defined by columns and topped with a coffered ceiling. Complementing the kitchen is a convenient walk-in pantry and center island with seating. An extra-large hearth room with gas fireplace and access to the rear deck provides a comfortable, family gathering place. The master bedroom, with a sloped ceiling, a spacious dressing area, and a luxurious whirlpool bath, offers a relaxing retreat. Split stairs located for family convenience introduces the spectacular lower level with a wine room, exercise room, wet bar, and two additional bedrooms.

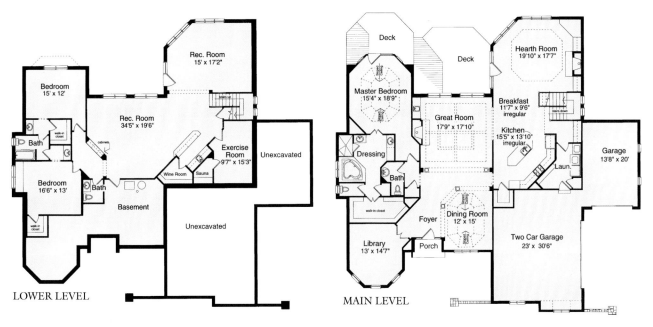

LOWER LEVEL

MAIN LEVEL

A stunning combination of both country and traditional exterior elements creates a timeless facade for this exquisite estate home. A dramatic two-story rotunda makes a grand first impression, followed by equally impressive dual staircases and a large great room with a cathedral ceiling and overlooking curved balcony and loft. The spacious kitchen easily serves the dining room, breakfast area, and great room. Note the walk-in pantry. The media/rec room features a wall of built-in cabinets to house television and stereo equipment. More oasis than bedroom, the master suite is enhanced by a deep tray ceiling and enjoys a fireplace, built-in dressing cabinetry, His and Hers walk-in closets, and a luxurious bath with every amenity. Two bedrooms, two baths, and an oversized bonus room are on the second floor.

plan# HPT9700120

STYLE: COUNTRY COTTAGE
FIRST FLOOR: 3,732 SQ. FT.
SECOND FLOOR: 1,080 SQ. FT.
TOTAL: 4,812 SQ. FT.
BONUS SPACE: 903 SQ. FT.
BEDROOMS: 4
BATHROOMS: 4½
WIDTH: 108' - 4"
DEPTH: 73' - 6"

SEARCH ONLINE @ EPLANS.COM

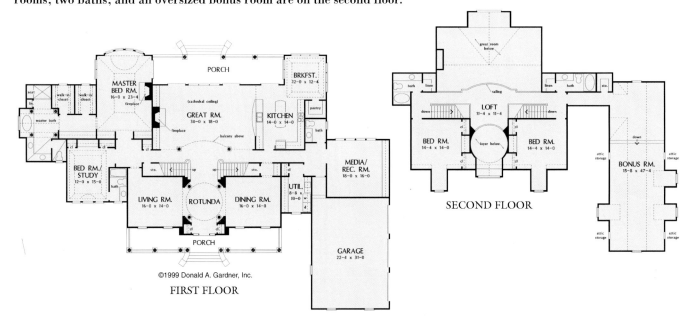

©1999 Donald A. Gardner, Inc.

FIRST FLOOR

SECOND FLOOR

B. NATHAN
© 1996 Donald A. Gardner Architects, Inc.

plan# HPT9700121

STYLE: COUNTRY
FIRST FLOOR: 2,920 SQ. FT.
SECOND FLOOR: 853 SQ. FT.
TOTAL: 3,773 SQ. FT.
BONUS SPACE: 458 SQ. FT.
BEDROOMS: 4
BATHROOMS: 3½
WIDTH: 78' - 7"
DEPTH: 75' - 7"

SEARCH ONLINE @ EPLANS.COM

This traditional farmhouse promises pleasurable living, indoors and out. The foyer is flanked by the formal dining room and living room/study. The cathedral-ceilinged great room is flooded with natural light from the rear porch and warmed by a raised-hearth fireplace. The adjacent kitchen and breakfast area enjoy their own side porch as well as a handy laundry/utility area. Away from the hustle and bustle of this work area lie the master bedroom and luxuriant bath, as well as another bedroom with walk-in closet and adjacent full bath. Upstairs, Bedrooms 2 and 3 share a full bath, creating a great space for kids.

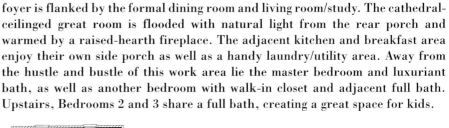

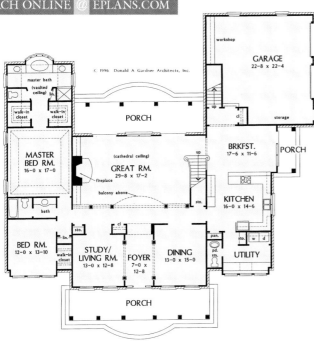

FIRST FLOOR

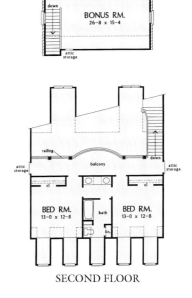

SECOND FLOOR

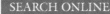

plan# **HPT9700122**

STYLE: COUNTRY COTTAGE
FIRST FLOOR: 2,568 SQ. FT.
SECOND FLOOR: 981 SQ. FT.
TOTAL: 3,549 SQ. FT.
BONUS SPACE: 385 SQ. FT.
BEDROOMS: 4
BATHROOMS: 4½
WIDTH: 66' - 8"
DEPTH: 71' - 0"
FOUNDATION: BASEMENT

SEARCH ONLINE @ EPLANS.COM

A smattering of architectual styles blends effortlessly to create this delightful two-story home. The foyer is flanked by the formal dining room and the living room. To the rear, the island kitchen and breakfast area enjoy a beamed ceiling bringing a bit of the rustic exterior inside. The family room offers a cozy space for informal gatherings with its warming fireplace. The master suite, with its whirlpool tub and shower with a built-in seat, sits on the far right; Bedroom 2, on the far left, would double easily as a guest room giving adequate privacy. Two additional bedrooms, each with a private bath, reside on the second floor as does space for a future rec room.

FIRST FLOOR

SECOND FLOOR

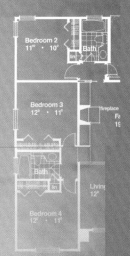

eplans.com

THE GATEWAY
TO YOUR NEW HOME

Looking for more plans? Got questions?
Try our one-stop home plans resource—eplans.com.

We'll help you streamline the plan selection process, so your dreams can become reality faster than you ever imagined. From choosing your home plan and ideal location to finding an experienced contractor, eplans.com will guide you every step of the way.

Mix and match! Explore! At eplans.com you can combine all your top criteria to find your perfect match. Search for your ideal home plan by any or all of the following:
> **Number of bedrooms or baths,**
> **Total square feet,**
> **House style,**
> **Designer, and**
> **Cost.**

With over 10,000 plans, the options are endless. Colonial, ranch, country, and Victorian are just a few of the house styles offered. Keep in mind your essential lifestyle features—whether to include a porch, fireplace, bonus room or main floor laundry room. And the garage—how many cars must it accommodate, if any? By filling out the preference page on eplans.com, we'll help you narrow your search. And, don't forget to enjoy a virtual home tour before any decisions are set in stone.

At eplans.com we'll make the building process a snap to understand. At the click of a button you'll find a complete building guide. And our eplan task planner will create a construction calendar just for you. Here you'll find links to tips and other valuable information to help you every step of the way—from choosing a site to moving day.

For your added convenience, our home plans experts are available for live, one-on-one chats at eplans.com. Building a home may seem like a complicated project, but it doesn't have to be—particularly if you'll let us help you from start to finish.

COPYRIGHT DOS & DON'TS

Blueprints for residential construction (or working drawings, as they are often called in the industry) are copyrighted intellectual property, protected under the terms of United States Copyright Law and, therefore, cannot be copied legally for use in building. However, we've made it easy for you to get what you need to build your home, without violating copyright law. Following are some guidelines to help you obtain the right number of copies for your chosen blueprint design.

COPYRIGHT DO

■ Do purchase enough copies of the blueprints to satisfy building requirements. As a rule for a home or project plan, you will need a set for yourself, two or three for your builder and sub-contractors, two for the local building department, and one to three for your mortgage lender. You may want to check with your local building department or your builder to see how many they need before you purchase. You may need to buy eight to 10 sets; note that some areas of the country require purchase of vellums (also called reproducibles) instead of blueprints. Vellums can be written on and changed more easily than blueprints. Also, remember, plans are only good for one-time construction.

■ Do consider reverse blueprints if you want to flop the plan. Lettering and numbering will appear backward, but the reversed sets will help you and your builder better visualize the design.

■ Do take advantage of multiple-set discounts at the time you place your order. Usually, purchasing additional sets after you receive your initial order is not as cost-effective.

■ Do take advantage of vellums. Though they are a little more expensive, they can be changed, copied, and used for one-time construction of a home. You will receive a copyright release letter with your vellums that will allow you to have them copied.

■ Do talk with one of our professional service representatives before placing your order. They can give you great advice about what packages are available for your chosen design and what will work best for your particular situation.

COPYRIGHT DON'T

■ Don't think you should purchase only one set of blueprints for a building project. One is fine if you want to study the plan closely, but will not be enough for actual building.

■ Don't expect your builder or a copy center to make copies of standard blueprints. They cannot legally—most copy centers are aware of this.

■ Don't purchase standard blueprints if you know you'll want to make changes to the plans; vellums are a better value.

■ Don't use blueprints or vellums more than one time. Additional fees apply if you want to build more than one time from a set of drawings. ■

hanley▲wood
HomePlanners

ORDERING IS EASY

HANLEY WOOD HOMEPLANNERS HAS EVERYTHING YOU NEED to build the home of your dreams, and with more than 50 years of experience in the industry, we make it as easy as possible for you to reach those goals. Just follow the steps on these pages and you'll receive a high-quality, ready-to-build set of home blueprints, plus everything else you need to make your home-building effort a success.

WHERE TO BEGIN?
1. CHOOSE YOUR PLAN

■ Browsing magazines, books, and eplans.com can be an exciting and rewarding part of the home-building process. As you search, make a list of the things you want in your dream home—everything from number of bedrooms and baths to details like fireplaces or a home office.

■ Take the time to consider your lot and your neighborhood, and how the home you choose will fit with both. And think about the future—how might your needs change if you plan to live in this house for five, 10, or 20 years?

■ With thousands of plans available, chances are that you'll have no trouble discovering your dream home. If you find something that's almost perfect, our Customization Program can help make it exactly what you want.

■ Most important, be sure to enjoy the process of picking out your new home!

WHAT YOU'LL GET WITH YOUR ORDER

Each designer's blueprint set is unique, but they all provide everything you'll need to build your home. Here are some standard elements you can expect to find in your plans:

1. FRONT PERSPECTIVE
This artist's sketch of the exterior of the house gives you an idea of how the house will look when built and landscaped.

2. FOUNDATION PLANS
This sheet shows the foundation layout including support walls, excavated and unexcavated areas, if any, and foundation notes. If your plan features slab construction rather than a basement, the plan shows footings and details for a monolithic slab. This page, or another in the set, may include a sample plot plan for locating your house on a building site.

3. DETAILED FLOOR PLANS
These plans show the layout of each floor of the house. Rooms and interior spaces are carefully dimensioned and keys are given for cross-section details provided later in the plans. The positions of electrical outlets and switches are shown.

4. HOUSE CROSS-SECTIONS
Large-scale views show sections or cutaways of the foundation, interior walls, exterior walls, floors, stairways, and roof details. Additional cross-sections may show important changes in floor, ceiling, or roof heights, or the relationship of one level to another. Extremely valuable during construction, these sections show exactly how the various parts of the house fit together.

5. INTERIOR ELEVATIONS
These elevations, or drawings, show the design and placement of kitchen and bathroom cabinets, laundry areas, fireplaces, bookcases, and other built-ins. Little extras, such as mantelpiece and wainscoting drawings, plus molding sections, provide details that give your home that custom touch.

6. EXTERIOR ELEVATIONS
Every blueprint set comes with drawings of the front exterior, and may include the rear and sides of your house as well. These drawings give necessary notes on exterior materials and finishes. Particular attention is given to cornice detail, brick, and stone accents or other finish items that make your home unique.

hanley▲wood
HomePlanners

ORDERING IS EASY

HANLEY WOOD
HOMEPLANNERS
ADVANTAGE
ORDER 24 HOURS!
1-800-521-6797

GETTING DOWN TO BUSINESS
2. PRICE YOUR PLAN

BLUEPRINT PRICE SCHEDULE

PRICE TIERS	1-SET STUDY PACKAGE	4-SET BUILDING PACKAGE	8-SET BUILDING PACKAGE	1-SET REPRODUCIBLE*
P1	$20	$50	$90	$140
P2	$40	$70	$110	$160
P3	$70	$100	$140	$190
P4	$100	$130	$170	$220
P5	$140	$170	$210	$270
P6	$180	$210	$250	$310
A1	$440	$490	$540	$660
A2	$480	$530	$580	$720
A3	$530	$590	$650	$800
A4	$575	$645	$705	$870
C1	$625	$695	$755	$935
C2	$670	$740	$800	$1000
C3	$715	$790	$855	$1075
C4	$765	$840	$905	$1150
L1	$870	$965	$1050	$1300
L2	$945	$1040	$1125	$1420
L3	$1050	$1150	$1240	$1575
L4	$1155	$1260	$1355	$1735
SQ1				.35/SQ. FT.

PRICES SUBJECT TO CHANGE   * REQUIRES A FAX NUMBER

plan
READY TO ORDER

Once you've found your plan, get your plan number and turn to the following pages to find its price tier. Use the corresponding code and the Blueprint Price Schedule above to determine your price for a variety of blueprint packages.

Keep in mind that you'll need multiple sets to fulfill building requirements, and only reproducible sets may be altered or duplicated.

To the right you'll find prices for additional and reverse blueprint sets. Also note in the following pages whether your home has a corresponding Deck or Landscape Plan, and whether you can order our Quote One® cost-to-build information or a Materials List for your plan.

IT'S EASY TO ORDER
JUST VISIT
EPLANS.COM OR CALL
TOLL-FREE
1-800-521-6797

PRICE SCHEDULE FOR ADDITIONAL OPTIONS

OPTIONS FOR PLANS IN TIERS P1-P6	COSTS
ADDITIONAL IDENTICAL BLUEPRINTS FOR "P1-P6" PLANS	$10 PER SET
REVERSE BLUEPRINTS (MIRROR IMAGE) FOR "P1-P6" PLANS	$10 FEE PER ORDER
1 SET OF DECK CONSTRUCTION DETAILS	$14.95 EACH
DECK CONSTRUCTION PACKAGE (INCLUDES 1 SET OF "P1-P6" PLANS, PLUS 1 SET STANDARD DECK CONSTRUCTION DETAILS)	ADD $10 TO BUILDING PACKAGE PRICE

OPTIONS FOR PLANS IN TIERS A1-SQ1	COSTS
ADDITIONAL IDENTICAL BLUEPRINTS IN SAME ORDER FOR "A1-L4" PLANS	$50 PER SET
REVERSE BLUEPRINTS (MIRROR IMAGE) WITH 4- OR 8-SET ORDER FOR "A1-L4" PLANS	$50 FEE PER ORDER
SPECIFICATION OUTLINES	$10 EACH
MATERIALS LISTS FOR "A1-C3" PLANS	$70 EACH
MATERIALS LISTS FOR "C4-SQ1" PLANS	$70 EACH

IMPORTANT EXTRAS	COSTS
ELECTRICAL, PLUMBING, CONSTRUCTION, AND MECHANICAL DETAIL SETS	$14.95 EACH; ANY TWO $22.95; ANY THREE $29.95; ALL FOUR $39.95
HOME FURNITURE PLANNER	$15.95 EACH
REAR ELEVATION	$10 EACH
QUOTE ONE® SUMMARY COST REPORT	$29.95
QUOTE ONE® DETAILED COST ESTIMATE (FOR MORE DETAILS ABOUT QUOTE ONE®, SEE STEP 3.)	$60

IMPORTANT NOTE
■ THE 1-SET STUDY PACKAGE IS MARKED "NOT FOR CONSTRUCTION."

Source Key
HPT97

PLAN #	PRICE TIER	PAGE	MATERIALS LIST	QUOTE ONE®	DECK	DECK PRICE	LANDSCAPE	LANDSCAPE PRICE	REGIONS
HPT9700001	SQ1	48	Y						
HPT9700002	SQ1	52	Y						
HPT9700003	SQ1	54	Y	Y			OLA028	P4	12345678
HPT9700004	L1	56	Y						
HPT9700005	SQ1	58							
HPT9700006	L1	60							
HPT9700007	SQ1	65							
HPT9700008	SQ1	66							
HPT9700009	SQ1	67							
HPT9700010	SQ1	68							
HPT9700011	SQ1	69	Y						
HPT9700012	L2	70							
HPT9700013	L2	71							
HPT9700014	L1	72	Y	Y					
HPT9700015	SQ1	73	Y						
HPT9700016	SQ1	74							
HPT9700018	SQ1	76							
HPT9700019	L1	77							
HPT9700020	SQ1	78	Y	Y					
HPT9700021	C3	79							
HPT9700022	SQ1	80	Y						
HPT9700023	SQ1	81	Y						
HPT9700024	C3	82							
HPT9700025	SQ1	83							
HPT9700026	C4	84	Y						
HPT9700027	SQ1	85							
HPT9700028	L2	86							
HPT9700029	SQ1	87							
HPT9700030	L1	88							
HPT9700031	SQ1	89							
HPT9700032	SQ1	90							
HPT9700033	L2	91							
HPT9700034	C4	92							
HPT9700035	L1	93							
HPT9700036	SQ1	94							
HPT9700037	SQ1	95	Y						
HPT9700038	SQ1	96	Y	Y					
HPT9700039	L1	97							
HPT9700040	SQ1	98							
HPT9700041	C4	99							
HPT9700042	L2	100	Y						
HPT9700043	C4	101	Y						
HPT9700044	SQ1	102	Y						
HPT9700045	L2	103	Y						
HPT9700046	L2	104							
HPT9700047	C4	105	Y	Y			OLA024	P4	123568
HPT9700048	SQ1	106					OLA017	P3	123568
HPT9700049	SQ1	107	Y	Y			OLA008	P4	1234568
HPT9700050	L3	108							
HPT9700051	SQ1	109					OLA014	P4	12345678
HPT9700052	SQ1	110	Y						
HPT9700053	L1	111	Y	Y			OLA037	P4	347
HPT9700054	SQ1	112	Y						
HPT9700055	L1	113							
HPT9700056	L1	114							
HPT9700057	SQ1	115							
HPT9700058	SQ1	116							
HPT9700059	SQ1	117							
HPT9700060	SQ1	118	Y						
HPT9700061	L1	119							
HPT9700062	L1	120							
HPT9700063	L1	121							
HPT9700064	L2	122							
HPT9700065	C4	123	Y						
HPT9700066	C3	124							
HPT9700067	L2	125							
HPT9700068	L1	126							
HPT9700069	L1	127							
HPT9700070	L3	128							
HPT9700071	C4	129							
HPT9700072	C4	130							
HPT9700073	C3	131							
HPT9700074	L2	132							
HPT9700075	L1	133							
HPT9700076	L2	134							
HPT9700077	SQ1	135	Y						
HPT9700078	L1	136							
HPT9700079	L1	137	Y	Y	ODA002	P2	OLA015	P4	123568

PLAN #	PRICE TIER	PAGE	MATERIALS LIST	QUOTE ONE®	DECK	DECK PRICE	LANDSCAPE	LANDSCAPE PRICE	REGIONS
HPT9700080	LI	138							
HPT9700081	SQI	139							
HPT9700082	LI	140				OLA008	P4	1234568	
HPT9700083	C4	141							
HPT9700084	LI	142							
HPT9700085	SQI	143							
HPT9700086	SQI	144	Y						
HPT9700087	SQI	145							
HPT9700088	SQI	146							
HPT9700089	SQI	147							
HPT9700090	SQI	148							
HPT9700091	SQI	149	Y						
HPT9700092	SQI	150	Y						
HPT9700093	C4	151	Y			OLA008	P4	1234568	
HPT9700094	SQI	152	Y						
HPT9700095	SQI	153							
HPT9700096	L3	154							
HPT9700097	C4	155							
HPT9700098	LI	156							
HPT9700099	SQI	157							
HPT9700100	SQI	158	Y						
HPT9700101	SQI	159	Y	Y					
HPT9700102	SQI	160	Y	Y					
HPT9700103	L3	161							
HPT9700104	L2	162							
HPT9700105	SQI	163							
HPT9700106	SQI	164							
HPT9700107	SQI	165							
HPT9700108	C4	166							
HPT9700109	SQI	167							
HPT9700110	SQI	168							
HPT9700111	SQI	169	Y						
HPT9700112	L2	170							
HPT9700113	LI	171							
HPT9700114	LI	172							
HPT9700115	SQI	173							
HPT9700116	L2	174							
HPT9700117	SQI	175	Y						
HPT9700118	C3	176	Y						

PLAN #	PRICE TIER	PAGE	MATERIALS LIST	QUOTE ONE®	DECK	DECK PRICE	LANDSCAPE	LANDSCAPE PRICE	REGIONS
HPT9700119	C4	177	Y						
HPT9700120	SQI	178	Y						
HPT9700121	SQI	179	Y						
HPT9700122	LI	180							
HPT9700123	SQI	62	Y			OLA008	P4	1234568	
HPT9700124	L2	75							

ORDER ONLINE AT EPLANS.COM

MORE TOOLS FOR SUCCESS
3. GET GREAT EXTRAS

WE OFFER A VARIETY OF USEFUL TOOLS THAT CAN HELP YOU THROUGH EVERY STEP OF THE home-building process. From our Materials List to our Customization Program, these items let you put our experience to work for you to ensure that you get exactly what you want out of your dream house.

MATERIALS LIST

For many of the designs in our portfolio, we offer a customized list of materials that helps you plan and estimate the cost of your new home. The Materials List outlines the quantity, type, and size of materials needed to build your house (with the exception of mechanical system items). Included are framing lumber, windows and doors, kitchen and bath cabinetry, rough and finished hardware, and much more. This handy list helps you or your builder cost out materials and serves as a reference sheet when you're compiling bids.

SPECIFICATION OUTLINE

This valuable 16-page document can play an important role in the construction of your house. Fill it in with your builder, and you'll have a step-by-step chronicle of 166 stages or items crucial to the building process. It provides a comprehensive review of the construction process and helps you choose materials.

QUOTE ONE®

The Quote One® system, which helps estimate the cost of building select designs in your zip code, is available in two parts: the Summary Cost Report and the Material Cost Report.

The Summary Cost Report, the first element in the package, breaks down the cost of your home into various categories based on building materials, labor, and installation, and includes three grades of construction: Budget, Standard, and Custom. Make even more informed decisions about your project with the second element of our package, the Material Cost Report. The material and installation cost is shown for each of more than 1,000 line items provided in the standard-grade Materials List, which is included with this tool. Additional space is included for estimates from contractors and subcontractors, such as for mechanical materials, which are not included in our packages.

If you are interested in a plan that does not indicate the availability of Quote One®, please call and ask our sales representatives, who can verify the status for you.

CUSTOMIZATION PROGRAM

If the plan you love needs something changed to make it perfect, our customization experts will ensure that you get nothing less than your dream home. Purchase a reproducible set of plans for the home you choose, and we'll send you our easy-to-use customization request form via e-mail or fax. For just $50, our customization experts will provide an estimate for your requested revisions, and once it's approved, that charge will be applied to your changes. You'll receive either five sets or a reproducible master of your modified design and any other options you select.

BUILDING BASICS

If you want to know more about building techniques—and deal more confidently with your subcontractors—we offer four useful detail sheets. These sheets provide non-plan-specific general information, but are excellent tools that will add to your understanding of Plumbing Details, Electrical Details, Construction Details, and Mechanical Details. These fact-filled sheets will help answer many of your building questions, and help you learn what questions to ask your builder and subcontractors.

HANLEY WOOD
HOMEPLANNERS
ADVANTAGE

ORDER 24 HOURS!
1-800-521-6797

HANDS-ON HOME FURNITURE PLANNER

Effectively plan the space in your home using our Hands-On Home Furniture Planner. It's fun and easy—no more moving heavy pieces of furniture to see how the room will go together. The kit includes reusable peel-and-stick furniture templates that fit on a 12"x18" laminated layout board—enough space to lay out every room in your house.

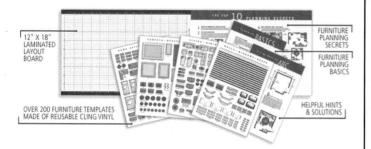

12" X 18" LAMINATED LAYOUT BOARD

FURNITURE PLANNING SECRETS

FURNITURE PLANNING BASICS

HELPFUL HINTS & SOLUTIONS

OVER 200 FURNITURE TEMPLATES MADE OF REUSABLE CLING VINYL

DECK BLUEPRINT PACKAGE

Many of the homes in this book can be enhanced with a professionally designed Home Planners Deck Plan. Those plans marked with a **D** have a corresponding deck plan, sold separately, which includes a Deck Plan Frontal Sheet, Deck Framing and Floor Plans, Deck Elevations, and a Deck Materials List. A Standard Deck Details Package, also available, provides all the how-to information necessary for building any deck. Get both the Deck Plan and the Standard Deck Details Package for one low price in our Complete Deck Building Package.

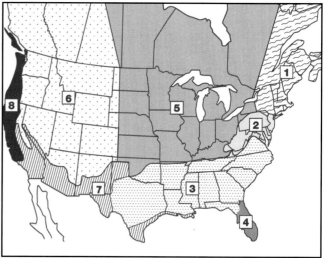

LANDSCAPE BLUEPRINT PACKAGE

Homes marked with an **L** in this book have a front-yard Landscape Plan that is complementary in design to the house plan. These comprehensive Landscape Blueprint Packages include a Frontal Sheet, Plan View, Regionalized Plant & Materials List, a sheet on Planting and Maintaining Your Landscape, Zone Maps, and a Plant Size and Description Guide. Each set of blueprints is a full 18" x 24" with clear, complete instructions in easy-to-read type.

Our Landscape Plans are available with a Plant & Materials List adapted by horticultural experts to eight regions of the country. Please specify from the following regions when ordering your plan:

Region 1: Northeast
Region 2: Mid-Atlantic
Region 3: Deep South
Region 4: Florida & Gulf Coast
Region 5: Midwest
Region 6: Rocky Mountains
Region 7: Southern California & Desert Southwest
Region 8: Northern California & Pacific Northwest

OUR EXCHANGE POLICY

With the exception of reproducible plan orders, we will exchange your entire first order for an equal or greater number of blueprints within our plan collection within **60 days** of the original order. The entire content of your original order must be returned before an exchange will be processed. Please call our customer service department at 1-888-690-1116 for your return authorization number and shipping instructions. If the returned blueprints look used, redlined, or copied, we will not honor your exchange. Fees for exchanging your blueprints are as follows: 20% of the amount of the original order, plus the difference in cost if exchanging for a design in a higher price bracket or less the difference in cost if exchanging for a design in a lower price bracket. (Reproducible blueprints are not exchangeable or refundable.) Please call for current postage and handling prices. Shipping and handling charges are not refundable.

ABOUT REPRODUCIBLES

Reproducibles (often called "vellums") are the most convenient way to order your blueprints. In any building process, you will need multiple copies of your blueprints for your builder, subcontractors, lenders, and the local building department. In addition, you may want or need to make changes to the original design. Such changes should be made only by a licensed architect or engineer. When you purchase reproducibles, you will receive a copyright release letter that allows you to have them altered and copied. You will want to purchase a reproducible plan if you plan to make any changes, whether by using our convenient Customization Program or going to a local architect.

ABOUT REVERSE BLUEPRINTS

Although lettering and dimensions will appear backward, reverses will be a useful aid if you decide to flop the plan. See Price Schedule and Plans Index for pricing.

ARCHITECTURAL AND ENGINEERING SEALS

Some cities and states now require that a licensed architect or engineer review and "seal" a blueprint, or officially approve it, prior to construction. Prior to application for a building permit or the start of actual construction, we strongly advise that you consult your local building official who can tell you if such a review is required.

ABOUT THE DESIGNS

The architects and designers whose work appears in this publication are among America's leading residential designers. Each plan was designed to meet the requirements of a nationally recognized model building code in effect at the time and place the plan was drawn. Because national building codes change from time to time, plans may not fully comply with any such code at the time they are sold to a customer. In addition, building officials may not accept these plans as final construction documents of record as the plans may need to be modified and additional drawings and details added to suit local conditions and requirements. Purchasers should consult a licensed architect or engineer, and their local building official, before starting any construction related to these plans.

LOCAL BUILDING CODES AND ZONING REQUIREMENTS

At the time of creation, these plans are drawn to specifications published by the Building Officials and Code Administrators (BOCA) International, Inc.; the Southern Building Code Congress International, (SBCCI) Inc.; the International Conference of Building Officials (ICBO); or the Council of American Building Officials (CABO). These plans are designed to meet or exceed national building standards. Because of the great differences in geography and climate throughout the United States and Canada, each state, county, and municipality has its own building codes, zone requirements, ordinances, and building regulations. Your plan may need to be modified to comply with local requirements. In addition, you may need to obtain permits or inspections from local governments before and in the course of construction. We authorize the use of the blueprints on the express condition that you consult a local licensed architect or engineer of your choice prior to beginning construction and strictly comply with all local building codes, zoning requirements, and other applicable laws, regulations, ordinances, and requirements. Notice: Plans for homes to be built in Nevada must be redrawn by a Nevada-registered professional. Consult your building official for more information on this subject.

TERMS AND CONDITIONS

These designs are protected under the terms of United States Copyright Law and may not be copied or reproduced in any way, by any means, unless you have purchased reproducibles which clearly indicate your right to copy or reproduce. We authorize the use of your chosen design as an aid in the construction of one single- or multi-family home only. You may not use this design to build a second or multiple dwellings without purchasing another blueprint or blueprints or paying additional design fees.

HOW MANY BLUEPRINTS DO YOU NEED?

Although a four-set building package may satisfy many states, cities, and counties, some plans may require certain changes. For your convenience, we have developed a reproducible plan, which allows you to take advantage of our Customization Program, or to have a local professional modify and make up to 10 copies of your revised plan. As our plans are all copyright protected, with your purchase of the reproducible, we will supply you with a copyright release letter. The number of copies you may need: 1 for owner, 3 for builder, 2 for local building department, and 1-3 sets for your mortgage lender.

DISCLAIMER

The designers we work with have put substantial care and effort into the creation of their blueprints. However, because we cannot provide on-site consultation, supervision, and control over actual construction, and because of the great variance in local building requirements, building practices, and soil, seismic, weather, and other conditions, **WE MAKE NO WARRANTY OF ANY KIND, EXPRESS OR IMPLIED, WITH RESPECT TO THE CONTENT OR USE OF THE BLUEPRINTS, INCLUDING BUT NOT LIMITED TO ANY WARRANTY OF MERCHANTABILITY OR OF FITNESS FOR A PARTICULAR PURPOSE. ITEMS, PRICES, TERMS, AND CONDITIONS ARE SUBJECT TO CHANGE WITHOUT NOTICE.**

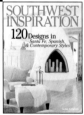

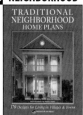

Home Planners wants your building experience to be as pleasant and trouble-free as possible.
That's why we've expanded our library of do-it-yourself titles to help you along.

31 NATURAL LIGHT

223 Sunny home plans
for all regions.
240 pgs. $8.95 NA

32 NOSTALGIA

100 Time-Honored
designs updated with
today's features.
224 pgs. $14.95 NOS

33 DREAM HOMES

50 luxury home plans.
Over 300 illustrations.
256 pgs. $19.95 SOD2

34 NARROW-LOT

245 versatile designs
up to 50 feet wide.
256 pgs. $9.95 NL2

35 SMALL HOUSES

Innovative plans for
sensible lifestyles.
224 pgs. $8.95 SM2

36 OUTDOOR

74 easy-to-build designs,
lets you create and build
your own backyard oasis.
128 pgs. $9.95 YG2

37 GARAGES

145 exciting projects from
64 to 1,900 square feet.
160 pgs. $9.95 GG2

38 PLANNER

A Planner for Building or
Remodeling your Home.
318 pgs. $17.95 SCDH

39 HOME BUILDING

Everything you need to know
to work with contractors
and subcontractors.
212 pgs. $14.95 HBP

40 RURAL BUILDING

Everything you need to
know to build your
home in the country.
232 pgs. $14.95 BYC

41 VACATION HOMES

Your complete guide
to building your
vacation home.
224 pgs. $14.95 BYV

42 DECKS

A brand new collection
of 120 beautiful and
practical decks.
144 pgs. $9.95 DP2

43 GARDENS & MORE

225 gardens, landscapes,
decks and more to
enhance every home.
320 pgs. $19.95 GLP

44 EASY-CARE

41 special landscapes
designed for beauty and
low maintenance.
160 pgs. $14.95 ECL

45 BACKYARDS

40 designs focused solely on
creating your own specially
themed backyard oasis.
160 pgs. $14.95 BYL

46 BEDS & BORDERS
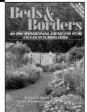
40 Professional designs
for do-it-yourselfers
160 pgs. $14.95 BB

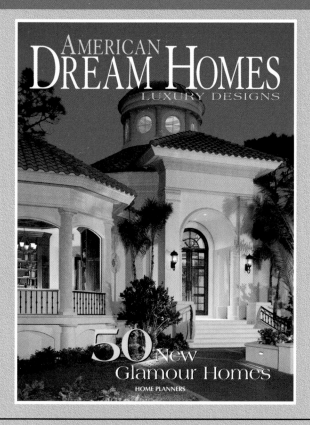
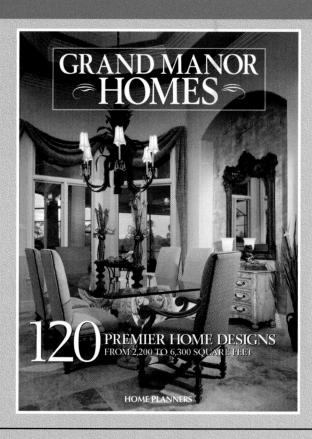
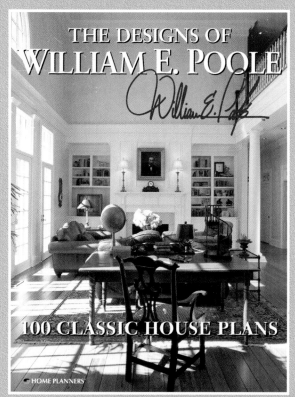